Participation without Politics

An analysis of the nature and the role of markets

SAMUEL BRITTAN

Published by

THE INSTITUTE OF ECONOMIC AFFAIRS

1975

First published April 1975

© THE INSTITUTE OF ECONOMIC AFFAIRS 1975

SBN 255 36067-3

Printed in Great Britain by
TONBRIDGE PRINTERS LTD,
Peach Hall Works, Tonbridge, Kent
Set in Intertype Baskerville

PREFACE

The *Hobart Papers* are intended to contribute a stream of authoritative, independent and lucid analysis to the understanding and application of economics to private and government activity. Their characteristic concern has been with the optimum use of scarce resources and the extent to which it can be achieved in the market within an appropriate legal/institutional framework to govern the buying and selling of goods or services.

Hobart Paper Special (62) has grown out of what was designed as a short Occasional Paper explaining the nature of 'the market' as understood by economists, its strengths and defects, based on passages from Mr Samuel Brittan's two most recent books (below). The extracts grew into a more substantial text now published as Part 2, 'Principles of the Market'. In addition, Mr Brittan has written a new discussion bringing the analysis up to date and applying it to current economic policy, which forms Part 1, 'Agenda for the Late 1970s'. Although the new material contains positive ('behaviourist') economic analysis it is mainly designed to indicate the implications for policy in Britain in 1975 and the immediate years ahead. Here Mr Brittan makes proposals that could be implemented by a government of any party, or a coalition. Perhaps they might be implemented more coherently by a new regrouping that may emerge from the increasing tensions within all parties between politicians who would use the market to raise living standards and those—Conservative or Labour paternalists—who see the market as giving too much power to the consumer and weakening the ability of the state to direct the use of resources.

The characteristic approach of the *Hobart Papers* has been to study the nature of markets and the reasons for their effectiveness or deficiencies. In particular they have investigated whether a 'market failure' was due to the inherent nature of the market or to avoidable defects in the institutional environment within which it is expected to work, and to consider which other arrangements might be superior. The nature of 'the market' is still widely and persistently misunderstood by laymen—from politicians and civil servants to lawyers and writers. It is here clarified by Mr Brittan in an exposition distinguished by simple

[3]

writing, clear thinking, and the unique authority derived from a blend of day-to-day economic observation and scrupulous scholarship. He argues that the market as a technical device for registering consumer preferences and apportioning scarce resources to satisfy them can be employed in a wide range of social and political circumstances and systems with private or socialised ownership of property. The extent to which it is effective or defective depends largely on the legal and institutional framework created by government and on public attitudes to the morality of its rewards and penalties. It can be frustrated in practice even where, as in Britain, it is intended to operate in principle. It has rules of the game that may be disagreeable, but without which it cannot yield its benefits. Mr Brittan indicates the 'corrections', largely to redistribute income and deal with externalities, required to make it serve the public interest. He argues that the market can be used to serve whichever purpose is desired, material goods or leisure, and that it is not in conflict with the urge to give.

The market has often been confused in public debate and associated with some schools of social philosophy rather than with others. Mr Brittan shows there is no such necessary association with politico-economic systems, capitalist, socialist or communist. Unreasoning fears of the market have prevented countries in varying stages of economic development from benefiting from it as an economic-technical instrument to record wants and allocate resources and as a source of information (to which economists have given increasing attention since a seminal article by Professor George Stigler[1] in 1961). Markets have been misused or abused (in a technical sense) in Western industrial societies, abused (in a pejorative sense) or not used (officially) in collectivist societies in Eastern Europe, and suppressed even where they have shown advantageous spontaneous growth in developing countries in Africa and Asia. The market is normally associated specifically with the English classical liberal school of economists from Adam Smith to Lionel Robbins, but it has been argued[2] that the writings of classical economists who broke away from the liberal tradition, such as Karl Marx, and of writers like Engels and Lenin who followed

[1] 'The Economics of Information', *Journal of Political Economy*, 1961.
[2] Raymond Fletcher, 'Reverse Income Tax: a Policy for Poverty', *Economic Age*, March-April 1970.

them in foreshadowing or devising collectivist economic systems, did not envisage or require the abolition of the market as an instrument for pricing and allocating scarce resources.

The post-war practices of countries in Eastern Europe that have increasingly used markets in varying forms have conflicted with the teaching of the older collectivist economists who condemned the market. The difficulties of allocating resources without markets have led East European economists—such as Liberman in Russia, Ota Šik of Czechoslovakia and Béla Csikós-Nagy of Hungary—to devise market systems.[1] And there has been increasing acknowledgement of the writings of Ludwig von Mises, F. A. Hayek, Lionel Robbins and others who for decades argued that markets could not effectively be replaced by centralised direction or by sophisticated computers.

The theoretical distinction (and confusion) between the market as a technical device and its institutional environment is clear enough. The important question for policy remains whether to work effectively the market requires decentralised ownership and disposal of the means of production or whether it can be incorporated into an economy where the means of production are owned in common, although controlled by central planners. The late Professor Ludwig von Mises was the leading proponent of the view, expounded in a celebrated article in 1920,[2] that rational economic calculus required market pricing which in a socialist economy was possible for consumer goods but not for the factors of production because they were not traded. This view was contested for several decades by economists since F. M. Taylor, H. D. Dickinson and others in the 1930s, who claimed that rational calculation could be incorporated into a socialist economy by a market mechanism. In more recent times it has been argued, most notably by the late Professor Oskar Lange, the distinguished Polish economist, that the computer could make the task easy. Mr Brittan argues

[1]Some of them are discussed in four IEA studies: Margaret Miller, Teresa M. Piotrowicz, Ljubo Sirc, Henry Smith, *Communist Economy under Change*, IEA, 1963; Margaret Miller, *Rise of the Russian Consumer*, IEA, 1965; Béla Csikós-Nagy, *Pricing in Hungary*, Occasional Paper 19, IEA, 1968; Ljubo Sirc, *Economic Devolution in Eastern Europe*, Longmans for the IEA, 1969. An early IEA text that discussed trade with East European countries was Alec Nove and Desmond Donnelly, *Trade with Communist Countries*, 1960.

[2]'Economic Calculation in the Socialist Commonwealth', *Archiv für Sozialwissenschaften*, 1920.

that the computer may help in static but not in dynamic conditions.[1]

In recent years Mises' early criticism has received more attention from economists in socialist economies.[2] Economists favourable to the view that the means of production should be owned in common differ among themselves on how far markets can be introduced into such a system. The view of a close student of collectivist economies, Professor Alec Nove, is that 'Change towards greater reliance on market elements will come, although 'Resistance to change is very strong in the political organs of the USSR ...'[3] The interesting question for economic policy on the use of the market in practice is whether change can come more readily in an economy where the means of production are owned in common but controlled at the centre or where both ownership and control are decentralised.

It may be that a reason for resistance to the use of the market is that the price it produces as its fulcrum has the same effect on income as that of a regressive tax: a given price takes a larger proportion of a lower than of a higher income. This view may explain the reluctance to use the market, especially for 'essential' goods or services such as education, medical care or housing. In turn it may also lead to a general dislike of the market as an insensitive instrument that bears disproportionately on people with relatively low incomes (or with disabilities that make them 'disadvantaged' or 'underprivileged'). Mr Brittan meets this objection with a proposal for a minimum income guarantee as the better solution than disrupting the price system and thereby losing its rationing and other functions. Here he goes beyond the IEA study group that in 1970 argued for a reverse income tax as a form of income guarantee.

The application of the market solution was graphically

[1]Professors F. A. Hayek and Lionel Robbins had maintained in the 1930s that the solution of the numerous simultaneous equations required for rational calculation was impossible without a market. In 1967 Lange replied: 'Let us put the simultaneous equations on an electronic computer and we shall obtain a solution in less than a second ... the electronic computer does not replace the market. It fulfils a function which the market was never able to perform.' ('The Computer and the Market', in C. Feinstein (ed.), *Capitalism, Socialism and Economic Growth*, Cambridge, 1967.)

[2]Professor Fritz Machlup in *Tribute to Mises*, Mount Pelerin Society, 1975.

[3]'Economic Reforms in the USSR and Hungary, a Study in Contrasts', in J. Chapman and Shun Msi-chou (eds.), *The Economics of the Communist World*, reprinted in Alec Nove and D. M. Nuti (eds.), *Socialist Economics*, Penguin Modern Economics Readings, 1972.

demonstrated by Miss Frances Cairncross in the *Guardian*, who showed the consequence of abolishing or impairing the market in what might be called socially sensitive commodities or services: milk, homes, sugar, coal, gas, electricity, oil.[1] She explained that suppressing or distorting the price that emerged from the market had the inevitable consequence of disturbing both supply and demand and produced consequences worse than those intended to be avoided. And, in terms of public policy, she reached the same conclusions as Mr Brittan: that it was better to supplement incomes rather than to depress prices: 'over every Cabinet Minister's chair should be inscribed the slogan "subsidise people not things" '.

If there is interest in the market as a mechanism in communist as well as capitalist countries, it is not surprising that it also crosses party boundaries in Britain. The Economics Editor of *The Times*, Mr Peter Jay, recently argued[2] that the market had both supporters and opponents in the two main political parties. Exponents of 'pro-market' monetary and fiscal management (as in Mr Denis Healey's control of the money supply), of private or government investment judged on returns, and of freeing international trade were found in both parties. And, equally, 'anti-market' industrial policies (such as those of Mr Anthony Wedgwood Benn, 'Mark I', and Mr Peter Walker), 'white elephants' such as Concorde, Maplin and the Channel Tunnel, import quotas and foreign exchange controls, were also supported by politicians in both parties. The attitude to the use of the market has no necessary identification with allegiance to British political parties, at least as they are now constituted. There is indeed on many fundamental issues more identity of outlook between wings of both parties than within them, and it may be that in the future more economically coherent political groupings will be formed round an understanding of the market as a convenient device for valuing and rationing scarce resources.

Mr Brittan also intriguingly examines the possible scope for markets in a society in which the urge to material consumption is replaced in some spheres by degrees of altruism. He argues that markets, which are commonly associated with the ac-

[1]'Subsidise People, not Things', *Guardian*, 28 October, 1974.
[2]*The Times*, 6 February, 1975.

quisitive society, can be used, with exceptions, whatever the basic motives that move men.

The *Paper* thus based on Mr Brittan's recent and new writing comprises a concise but stimulating explanation of the market that will educate the newcomer to economics and edify the practical man (or woman) in industry, government and communications who uses or judges markets, as well as students and teachers of economics who have been brought up to regard the market as unimportant, unnecessary or undesirable.

Readers of this Hobart Paper Special will wish to consult Mr Brittan's more extensive discussion of the central and associated themes in his two books: *Capitalism and the Permissive Society* and *Is there an Economic Consensus?*, published by Macmillan, 1973, whom we thank for permission to use the extracts on which Part 2 is based.

February 1975   EDITOR

CONTENTS

PREFACE   3

THE AUTHOR   12

ACKNOWLEDGEMENTS   12

PART 1—Agenda for the Late 1970s

I INTRODUCTION   15
    Methods of co-operation
    Purpose of the *Paper*
    The 'real' questions

II RESULTS OF SUPPRESSING MARKETS   18
    Effects of subsidies
    Non-price rationing
    The housing muddle
    Not willing the means

III PROPOSALS TO MAKE MARKETS WORK   22
    Secondary markets—*or* In praise of black markets
    The sale of leases—a new market
    Legalise money transactions; tax releasings

IV THE STATE AND ENTERPRISE   25
    The wrong case for profits
    The company crisis
    Attitudes to private enterprise
    An alternative to the NEB
    Industrial co-operatives

V 'VOICE' AND 'EXIT'   32
    Voting with one's feet

VI NEW THINKING FROM THE NEW WORLD   35
    An impoverished discussion
    Five new developments
    Weaknesses of the political market-place

[9]

VII OLD THINKING FROM THE OLD WORLD   39
    Pressure group influences
    'Consumerism'

VIII NEW MARKETS TO SOLVE NEW PROBLEMS   41
    Conventional interventionism
    The premature end of growth
    Inflation—the less obvious effects
    Indexation—second best, but vital

IX POINTERS FOR POLICY   46

Part 2—Principles of the Market

I THE MARKET IN THEORY   51
    Judging the market economy
    Opinion among economists
    The five requirements of economic society
    Can computers replace the market?
    Does the market fabricate wants?
    Choice—a burden to be delegated?
    Poverty and equality
    Discrimination and poverty
    Pressure groups and government

II USES AND ABUSES OF THE MARKET ECONOMY   61
    Market economy, price mechanism, capitalism
    Trade and the 'zero-sum' game
    The invisible hand
    Externalities (neighbourhood effects)
    Public goods
    Government intervention—the onus of proof
    The price mechanism
    Perfect competition
    Short-period and long-period adjustments
    Free markets and the price mechanism
    Safety valves
    Government use of the price mechanism
    Pricing and standards
    Economists and the price mechanism
    The price mechanism and the public

III THE CORRECTED MARKET ECONOMY   77
    Freedom or prosperity?
    Value of fringe markets
    Compensating the victims of change
    Intervention in labour markets
    Incompatibility of reward by merit and equality
    Payment by merit and direction of labour

IV MARKET ECONOMY—CAPITALIST OR SOCIALIST?   87
    Coping with static or dynamic conditions
    Nationalised industry and competition
    A market in intellectual property

V THE ROLE OF ECONOMICS—POSITIVE OR NORMATIVE?   93
    The competence of the economist
    Economics without price (and without markets)
    Growth models in industrialised and developing
        countries
    Material wealth and choice
    Economic efficiency is subjective
    Value and value-judgements
    Markets, straitjackets, and the collapse of constraints

VI BEYOND THE PURITAN ETHIC—   99
    THE ECONOMICS OF SELLING AND GIVING
    Altruism and the market
    Maximising giving by maximising income
    Selective and indiscriminate giving
    Profit and higher ideals
    Rejection of material consumption
    Monopoly resistance to minority preferences
    Static consumption and population
    Keynes and the 10-hour week society
    Function of money and markets
    Surplus goods, scarce work
    'Non-economic' goods
    'Free' goods
    A guarantee of minimum income/reverse income tax
    Markets without the puritan ethic

[11]

VII CONCLUDING NOTES 113
    Self-interest and the public interest
    Beliefs—reasons and validity
    Capitalism and rationality
    Understanding the price mechanism
    The dilemma of the economic liberal
    Forms of market economy

QUESTIONS FOR DISCUSSION 120

FURTHER READING 123

THE AUTHOR

SAMUEL BRITTAN was born in 1933 and educated at Kilburn Grammar School and Jesus College, Cambridge, where he took First-Class Honours in economics. He then held various posts on the *Financial Times* (1955-61); was Economics Editor of the *Observer* (1961-64); an Adviser at the Department of Economic Affairs (1965); and has been principal economic commentator on the *Financial Times* since 1966.

He was the first winner of the Senior Wincott Award for financial journalists in 1971. He was a Research Fellow of Nuffield College in 1973-74 and in 1974 was elected a Visiting Fellow.

His publications include *Steering the Economy* (third edition, Penguin, 1971), *Left or Right: The Bogus Dilemma* (Secker & Warburg, 1968), *The Price of Economic Freedom: A Guide to Flexible Rates* (Macmillan, 1970), *Is There An Economic Consensus?* (Macmillan, 1973), and *Capitalism and the Permissive Society* (Macmillan, 1973). For the IEA he has written *Government and the Market Economy* (Hobart Paperback No. 2, 1971), and a contribution to *Crisis '75 . . . ?* (Occasional Paper Special (No. 43), January 1975).

ACKNOWLEDGEMENTS

A special word of thanks is due to Arthur Seldon, whose idea the whole project was, and without whose continuing help and encouragement it would never have reached fruition.

I am also extremely grateful to Ralph Harris for suggesting the title and to Michael Solly for indispensable editorial assistance.

S.B.

[12]

PART I

Agenda for the Late 1970s

PART 1

Agenda for the Late 1970s

I. INTRODUCTION

Methods of co-operation

There are three known ways in which people can be brought to co-operate for their mutual benefit. First, they can be given orders—*the command system,* which remains a command system even if those who give the orders are elected by the shop floor or the commands are determined by majority vote. Secondly, they can do what is required out of mutual benevolence—*unenforced good behaviour.* Thirdly, they can co-operate because it is in their private interest to provide others with what they require—*the market system.*

Benevolence is rarely sufficient outside very small groups such as families. Not merely does it fail to provide sufficient *incentive* in wide groupings; it does not provide sufficient information. Even if we were all prepared to do the best for our fellow citizens out of mutual love, it is not immediately obvious *which* goods and services they want, *who* would be best employed providing which of them, and by which *methods.* A command economy also faces such an information problem; but if those who give the orders are prepared to impose their preferences on others, the lack of information is to that degree less serious.

All societies use all three principles—commands, unenforced good behaviour and the market. The market has the advantage of providing both the information and the incentives for a system of *non-coercive co-operation.* But if it is to operate it requires a framework of rules and conventions which ultimately rely on the force of the state. This framework is quite different from and additional to governmental action to supplement the market and 'correct' its adverse side-effects.

Conversely, not even the most powerful and well-informed government can manage without some mutually profitable exchange to oil the wheels, and without a feedback of information from the market-place. Moreover a minimum of mutual goodwill is required to cope with the many human situations which cannot be covered by orders, rules or contracts. Indeed even state force itself is in the last resort dependent on goodwill. For as David Hume remarked:[1]

[1]*Essay on the First Principles of Government* (1741–42), in *Essays Moral, Political and Literary,* modern edn., OUP, 1963.

'The governors have nothing to support them but opinion. The Sultan of Egypt or the Emperor of Rome might drive his harmless subjects like brute beasts, against their sentiments and inclination; but he must at least have led his mamelukes or praetorian bands like men, by their opinion.'

It is of course not easy, in complex societies, to say whose opinion counts and to what extent.

Purpose of the Paper

Different people will put a different emphasis on the relative importance of commands, market incentives and mutual benevolence. None of the three methods can be dismissed as immoral —it is how they are used, and for what purpose, that determines their morality.

This *Paper* is concerned with the role of markets in harnessing private aims for the public good. People who place a high value on individuals being free to choose their occupation, lifestyle and consumption pattern should place a special value on the market system. But as markets will always exist in some form, in the open or underground if suppressed by government, their working should be of concern to people of all views.

The key signalling device of the market is prices—not the *average* index which appears in headlines about 'rising prices', but the price of one product or service *relative* to another. Prices act both as a method of rationing scarce goods or labour (or foreign exchange—the sterling rate is a price) and as a signal and an incentive to supply whatever is in most demand by the members of society.

This distinction between average and relative prices is fundamental in economic analysis and policy. Macro-economic theory and macro-economic 'models' concentrate on broad totals such as national output, exports, or imports and, at best, on indices of average prices. Study of these aggregates is essential to understand the environment—whether boom or slump, inflation or deflation—in which individual markets work. But macro-economic models (especially those emanating from Cambridge or from the ambience of the Treasury) are always in danger of underplaying the role of individual markets and prices, such as the foreign exchange or labour market, and even of neglecting the role of monetary forces in determining average prices in the longer term. Moreover, there will always remain something unsatisfactory about such models until they can be linked to the 'micro' choices facing individual workers, employers, consumers and savers.[1]

A common fallacy is to suppose that markets and prices are of interest only to people who believe in self-regulating systems. As is shown repeatedly in this *Paper*, market incentives can be used as instruments of government intervention and regulation, e.g. by adjusting some prices or putting a price on non-priced, and therefore wastefully used, resources (such as rivers or radio waves). Nor do markets presuppose a 'capitalist' system. State-owned enterprises (as in fuel or education) or workers' co-operatives (like Meriden) must have instruments of co-ordination and methods of ascertaining consumer preference. Eastern European countries have experimented with various types of market socialism—although whether the full benefits of a market system can be obtained without a substantial private enterprise sector is one of the questions to be discussed (pp. 87–92). Nor does the acceptance of markets as an instrument of allocation mean that we must accept the resulting distribution of income and wealth—although again how far we can go in redistribution, and the best methods to employ, are difficult and controversial questions (pp. 84–87).

Perhaps the most irritating of all fallacies is the view that a market system is necessarily highly materialist. Any system will reflect the values and interests of those who operate it. There is, of course, a feedback effect; but it is much exaggerated by opponents of markets who regard their fellow citizens as helpless automatons, responding uncritically to every advertising and media message, with no capacity to learn from experience. In Part 2, VI, of this *Paper*, there is an extended discussion of how markets can be used in a society which has gone beyond the puritan ethic to a 'less materialist' outlook.

The 'real' questions

To most people economic problems mean subjects to do with money, such as inflation, unemployment (as aggravated by government monetary mismanagement) and the balance of pay-

---

[1] A notable pioneering effort in this direction is E. S. Phelps et al, *Microeconomic Foundations of Employment and Inflation Theory*, Macmillan, 1971; see also Milton Friedman's IEA Lecture on a reconsideration of the Phillips Curve, Occasional Paper 44, 1975.

ments. But we should never forget that the main questions facing society are 'real', not monetary.

—What is the most humane and efficient way of co-ordinating the activities of the 90 per cent plus of the working population in employment, so that they can supply the expressed needs of their fellow citizens with the minimum of tension and conflict?

—What should we do with 'lame-duck' industries or firms?

—How much reliance should we place on the profit motive?

—What is the scope for private and collective decision in education, health, housing and pensions?

—What is the most effective way of helping the poor?

—How do we distinguish between redistribution towards the underdogs and sheer envy of the top dogs (often wrongly identified)?

These are some fundamental problems which will always be with us. Of course they link up with the problems of inflation and unemployment, but they cannot be explained only by their monetary aspects: for example, unemployment can be caused by too slow adaptation to changes in tastes or techniques that have nothing to do with monetary causes.

Indeed one of the least remarked, but most insidious, costs of rapid inflation is that it enormously increases public misunderstanding of, and hostility towards, the price mechanism as a source of incentives and a method of allocation of resources. It would be a fair guess that most people confronted with the word 'prices' think of the 'cost of living', which, so it seems to them, always goes up and adds to the problems of life. Changes in *relative* prices, which are necessary to guide production and consumption, thereby become confused with the upward movement of the *general average* of prices associated with currency debasement.

II. RESULTS OF SUPPRESSING MARKETS

Effects of subsidies

It is in this general climate that a clamour for subsidies, especially for 'essentials', develops. Unfortunately, subsidies are ways of treating the symptoms which make the disease worse. If a product, say sugar, is scarce, a high 'relative' price signals to people the amount of other goods that have to be foregone to pay for a pound of sugar whose price has risen, perhaps because of what is happening in world markets. A subsidy, by contrast, encourages profligate spending precisely when the need is for economy. It is moreover a peculiar redistribution of income which favours consumers with an above-average taste for sugar, rich and poor alike, and (because of its tax cost) penalises consumers with average or below-average tastes or requirements.

If the (relative) price of a product which looms largest in the budget of poor families rises, they will indeed suffer. Increased cash benefits are, however, a much more efficient way of helping them than keeping the price down by subsidies. If cash benefits are of the right size they can restore the real income of the relatively poor while still encouraging economy in the use of the scarce product among all sections, and avoiding the spillover benefits for people who do not need the subsidies.

The food subsidies, which at the beginning of 1975 were running at an annual rate of over £600 million, illustrate these propositions. Let us assume they were financed from the increase in the basic and higher-income tax rates in the 1974 Budget. On that basis the above-£70 a week income group did contribute about £140 million more than it received. But so far from this sum being concentrated among the poorest families, the middle-income groups secured the lion's share, £100 million when subsidies were 'netted out' against tax. The effect on income distribution was almost identical to that of raising the tax rates and distributing £11 per head in cash to everyone, tycoon as well as tailor.[1]

Non-price rationing

The high cost of subsidies is one of several reasons often advanced for coupon rationing. Import quotas are another form of coupon rationing, advocated to reduce the cost of subsidising the sterling exchange rate above its free market level (the subsidies here are paid either from the reserves or from official overseas borrowing). The supposed requirement 'to save energy' is another pretext. But perhaps the strongest urge behind the talk of rationing is to promote a psychological shock 'to bring home to people the seriousness of the situation'. Even for this purpose

[1]Christopher Ritson, 'Who gets a subsidy?', *New Society*, 23 January, 1975.

there is a confusion between the psychological requirements of total military war and those of prolonged economic weakness, where commercial imagination, initiative and incentive may be of more use than 'fairly shared' austerity.

In a world of scarcity some form of rationing is always with us. Rationing by coupon has the disadvantage of ignoring the different (and changing) tastes and circumstances of different people and firms. Import quotas must be allocated on an arbitrary basis, such as past use or current output, which ignores the continuing day-by-day process of technological and market change and thereby tends to ossify the industrial structure. We have seen that there are more efficient ways of redistributing resources between income groups, while, within a given income group, coupon rationing discriminates against people with certain preferences and in favour of those with others.

Just as important, rationing is a form of coercion, forbidding people from spending their incomes in ways they prefer. This can be most clearly seen if we imagine a world in which everything is rationed. Then money left after buying the 'ration' of food, clothing, etc. is useless, and everybody is compelled to adopt the same life-style irrespective of preferences, and forbidden to spend his income in any except one way approved by the powers that be, whoever they are.

The housing muddle

The worst advertisement for rationing by administrative allocation is the market in rented housing. With rents so far below free market levels, private rented housing is not available on the market, while council houses are allocated by local authorities under a 'waiting list' system. The result is a serious misallocation of house room and an arbitrary redistribution of incomes, with many low-rent council homes in the possession of tenants a good deal better off than people who do not have such good fortune. The incentive to build for rent or even let out spare rooms is killed off, and many people who would pay the market rent are homeless.

The practical consequences have been spelt out by Mr David Eversly, the former chief strategic planner to the GLC:

'. . . no unfurnished rented property is now available, and furnished rooms only at exorbitant rents . . . newcomers to the

[20]

housing market are under more of a disadvantage than they once were.'

Homelessness is on the increase.

'Local authorities are putting more people into bed and breakfast accommodation, and organisations catering for the young single homeless report a great increase in business. What this means is that local authority housing departments have no means of dealing with a section of the population who, a generation ago, would have found transitional accommodation in the private market . . .'

Private tenancies are increasingly a privilege for

'those who need [them] least (just examine the National Trust's rent roll). . . . what are we going to do to enable people to move house when they need to change jobs? What are we going to offer, besides a council house after a very long wait, to young couples getting married and perhaps wanting to start a family? If the answer is "nothing", then no one should be surprised if large cities cannot man their essential services, if homelessness is on the increase, and if fertility is falling faster than even the optimistic had demanded.'[1]

How many fires, floods and plagues would have wrought the havoc created by gradual destruction of the house-letting market by rent restriction since 1915?

Not willing the means

It is important to see what has gone wrong. Housing subsidies, whether for tenants or owner-occupiers, can be justified if it is believed that people cannot be trusted to spend enough on homes for themselves and their families. (Help for poorer families is not itself a sufficient justification.) But having made this paternalist judgement, central and local governments (and voters who elected them) have not willed the means.

If the public authorities were prepared to build enough houses and flats to supply to the full the extra demand created by their rent policies, more of the nation's resources would go into

[1]'Landlords' slow goodbye', *New Society*, 16 January, 1975.

housing than citizens desire. But this would be the limit of state coercion; and once sufficient accommodation were built, rented housing would be available, like any other goods or services, without queueing or administrative allocation. A *permanent* housing shortage, and the power of public officials over individual lives, arises because a political commitment to rent (i.e. house-price) ceilings in no way carries with it a parallel commitment by central or local government to build sufficient houses to satisfy the demand created by these below-market ceilings. The politicians have fixed the price without filling the resulting gap between supply and demand. This is an example of the imperfections of the political process, discussed below (pp. 37–42).

III. PROPOSALS TO MAKE MARKETS WORK

Secondary markets—or *In praise of black markets*

Political economists who emphasise the usefulness of pricing and markets are frequently accused both of having a debased view of human nature and of assuming an ideal world! After two hundred years since Adam Smith's *Wealth of Nations* (1776), they should have learned to live with both charges.

In the real world, pricing has much to contribute to the 'economics of the second best'. A starting point is the principle that, *if rationing by coupons or quotas is 'politically inevitable', the coupons and quotas should be transferable between individuals and firms at mutually agreed prices.* So far from being condemned as 'black market', such transactions should be recognised as increasing both the efficiency of allocation and the range of human choice. Let us consider a transfer of confectionery coupons between a charlady and a duchess, or of the right to buy subsidised EEC butter between a pensioner and a prosperous suburban housewife. No-one benefits from forbidding such a secondary market. The charlady and the pensioner prefer the other things they can buy with the money proceeds of the confectionery or butter coupons they sell. Otherwise they would not sell them. Forbidding such transactions makes the poor poorer than they otherwise would be.

That this is often a *very* second-best system can be seen from the extreme case of the frequently advocated 'white market' in petrol coupons. Although far better than a fixed ration for all, it represents a redistribution of income in favour of motorists whose desire to drive is below average—which is an odd kind of redistribution to make. Discouragement for voracious motorists can be made as high as desired[1] by putting up the price of petrol sufficiently. Even with the confectionery and butter coupons, the gainers are the pensioners and charladies who do not desire to take up their allocation—who are not the same as the poorest, although the categories obviously overlap. Straight cash redistribution financed from taxation could be more effectively concentrated on pensioners and others who need it most.

The sale of leases—a new market

A secondary market in 'rationed' services would probably be of most value in rented housing. The defects of below-market council rents, irrespective of means, could be mitigated if council tenants were empowered to sell their rights to dwell in the property on short- or long-term leases. (The Conservatives have merely proposed that council tenants should be empowered to *buy* their houses at below-market prices.) This reform would release to the market many houses too large or otherwise not really required by council tenants, but clung onto at present because of the high cost of moving. A secondary market of this kind would undoubtedly bring down house prices and reduce 'key money' in the private rented sector.

At present a council tenant can arrange a mutual exchange ('MX') with another tenant but only with the consent of both local authorities. Some local authorities run exchange bureaux, and advertisements are placed in local newspapers. But as financial transactions between parties are not permitted, the system works only if there is a rare double coincidence of 'wants': A must want B's dwelling (taking into account size, quality and location) and B must want A's. (This is rather like a textbook description of a barter economy before the invention of money.) Not surprisingly, this restriction does not produce much mobility. About 20 per cent of the tenants of both the

[1]Not desired by me. A brief argument for disbelief in the energy crisis is stated in my contribution to *Crisis '75..?*, Occasional Paper Special (No. 43), IEA, 1975.

[23]

GLC and Newcastle are on the transfer list at any one time, but only 3 per cent are transferred and less than $\frac{1}{2}$ per cent through 'MX'.[1]

Legalise money transactions; tax releasings

A so-called scandal recently came to light in the London borough of Tower Hamlets where immigrant families 'desperate for accommodation' were 'jumping the housing queue by buying council rent books'. One family was reported to have paid £460 for a flat and another £800, in addition to the normal weekly rent which they continued to pay to the Council.[2] The Press report showed a photograph of the eviction of a family who had lived for two years in a flat acquired in this way. They were 'being interviewed by a social worker and were now in council care'.

Would the legalisation of such transactions hit the people at the bottom of existing council lists? The answer is 'Only if the outgoing tenant would have departed in any event'. If it was the financial consideration that induced him to move, both he and the new tenant are better off and no-one is worse off. But to cover the proportion of outgoing tenants who would have left in any event, and thereby released accommodation for new tenants selected by the council, a tax could be imposed on releasings. There would always be some rate of tax on releasings which would make it possible for councils to increase subsidised house building, or pay cash grants to poorer families, sufficient to compensate for any net loss in their free housing stock, while at the same time improving the mobility (and therefore welfare) of existing tenants.

The main reform required if such a secondary market is to be located is a clear definition of the terms of existing council tenancies. At the moment they have no definite length of life and their disposition on the departure of a tenant (whether to a member of the previous family or not) is within the discretion of the local council, which means, in day-to-day practice, officials. Should they thus be given such enormous power over the lives of their fellow-men? The creation of markets would strengthen the citizen against the official.

[1] Information kindly supplied by Heather Bird of the Centre for Environmental Studies.
[2] 'Council flats for sale at up to £800', *Evening Standard,* 13 February, 1974.

IV. THE STATE AND ENTERPRISE

The wrong case for profits

Markets and prices are important as signals and incentives for producers as well as a means of allocation among consumers. The case for profits is often put in entirely the wrong terms, such as a source of funds to finance investment, or to provide savings for industry.

If this were the main case, a completely collectivist system could do as well. If freeing resources for investment is the main requirement, all that is necessary is that a gap be created between total production and private and public consumption. Taxation and a budget surplus will do just as well for this purpose as company profits. Whether the state then invests itself or lends conditionally through a National Enterprise Board becomes secondary. The potentialities of collective saving have never been better demonstrated than in Stalin's Russia, where the investment (or savings) ratio far exceeded anything achieved in capitalist countries.

The real value of the profit yardstick is as a *criterion* to guide investment in the direction of customer requirements, home and export, as well as a source of information about the efficiency of alternative techniques and methods. In a world of change and uncertainty, some firms will make abnormally high profits and others low profits (or losses).

Both the signals and the incentives are atrophied in the present-day climate of opinion, where high profits are stigmatised as 'obscene' and losses as 'failing the nation', and as an excuse for nationalisation. Moreover, no better method of discouraging risk-taking than price controls has been devised. Why go for an untried process or product, and all the heartaches involved, if success in the form of high profits is suppressed by the Price Commission *while failure continues to carry a penalty?* All the incentives are to play safe and avoid trouble.

The company crisis

It is well known that, from the second half of 1974 onwards, a crisis of profitability and 'liquidity' (which in plain English usually means credit-worthiness) affected a large number of companies and not merely an unsuccessful few. One main group of causes was an inflation-blind system of corporate taxation and price control which treated paper profits, out of which stocks and capital equipment have to be replaced, as if they were real. A large part of the evils of even the worst system of corporate taxation would however eventually be overcome by passing taxation on in final prices, until the corporate sector as a whole was able to earn a sufficient return on capital to service its debts and make a 'normal' (market) return on capital. It is price control that is the more important inhibition, and on which the main attack should be made.

A second group of causes is that connected with recession. Profits are a volatile form of income, which rise disproportionately in a boom and fall disproportionately in a slump. Unfortunately, once inflation has gained a certain momentum, it is impossible to curb it, or perhaps even prevent it accelerating, without a period of depressed business activity during which both employment and profits are hit. This is one of the most important reasons for not going in for inflationary policies in the first place. The combination of rising prices and slump is not a crisis of capitalism but the nemesis of so-called 'Keynesian economics'—the doctrine that money supply and the budget balance do not matter so long as unemployment is above some politically-set target.

It is hardly surprising that the private capital market should have dried up in 1974, when current profits were depressed, credit (quite rightly) tight, and when both the borrower and the lender in any fixed-interest-rate contract had to take a gamble, both on the likely long-term rate of inflation and on whether the price control authorities would allow a profit to be made on an otherwise successful venture. Yet the collectivists have the effrontery to cite the state of the capital market as a proof of the failure of 'capitalism'—a 'proof' which all too many of our salaried non-entrepreneurial 'industrial statesmen' believe. There is a moral case to be made (and answered) against the private ownership of the means of production, but on both sides the present argument is being carried forward in a thoroughly trivialised manner.

Attitudes to private enterprise

Supporters of a competitive private enterprise market economy have drawn comfort from surveys showing that a majority of 'workers' are against more nationalisation or any large extension of government controls. But economists who emphasise the 'competitive' and 'market' aspects of such an economy should not be over-sanguine. Some 69 per cent of the sample questioned in one such survey thought it 'should be the object of the government to help British companies'. To remove any ambiguity, 54 per cent thought that this should take the form of 'financial help' or 'lending money to firms when they need it', and most of the others wanted cash assistance in one guise or another.[1]

It is doubtful if most people in the poll realised that *they* would be providing, as taxpayers, the resources for this 'help' Politicians and economists who are sceptical of open-ended rescue-operations for 'lame-duck' industries are customarily reviled as 'right wing' and even (such is the debasement of language) as 'anti-liberal'. The essential point, rarely grasped, is that citizens are being coerced by the tax system to support the car, electronics, aircraft and many other industries at a scale they are not prepared to support from their own pockets as consumers.

Whatever else can be claimed for the National Enterprise Board (NEB), the 'regeneration of industry' is no more likely than from previous industrial intervention by governments of all parties. If there is a shortage of entrepreneurial skill, or knowledge, or expertise related to particular industries, why should the creation of a new central body bring them into existence?

Mr Geoffrey Owen, the Deputy Editor of the *Financial Times* and a former Industrial Reorganisation Corporation (IRC) official, has taken mechanical engineering as an example of the difficulties facing the new Board.

'. . . in most sectors success depends on technical factors, stemming from the design of the product, which are not easy for an outsider to appraise. To discover whether Weir, for example, is drawing ahead of or falling behind its foreign competitors in pump technology would require a lengthy study of world markets, technical developments in Germany, and so on. Even if the conclusion were that there is a weakness which needs to be corrected, is the NEB any better placed to put it right than the company itself? . . .

'The whole [industry] has in fact been thoroughly tramped

[1]ORC (Opinion Research Centre) Poll, *The Times*, 13 and 14 January, 1975.

over during the past 15 years or so by assorted investigators from the Ministry of Technology, the IRC, the Little Neddy and other agencies (with the prize for prompting the largest number of reports probably going to machine tools). Some of these studies have identified, in fairly general terms, the ingredients that make for a successful engineering business, and they have played a useful educational role within the industry. What they have not done is provide any support for the idea that active intervention by an outside agency like the NEB would make more than a marginal difference to the industry's performance.'[1]

Mr Owen's conclusion is that the NEB should concentrate on its task of managing the very extensive portfolio of investments which it will inherit from previous government interventions. These include aircraft engines, computers, machine tools, motor cycles, cars (with probably a large stake in British Leyland), trucks, construction equipment and electronics.

As Mr Owen remarks :

'This is surely enough to satisfy those in the Labour Party who favour competitive public enterprise as a counterweight and spur to the private sector. Several of the companies which will be controlled by the NEB have severe problems but also great commercial opportunities. If the NEB can demonstrate that it is making a better job of these investments than the previous managements and owners (and this will take some years), then and only then will it be appropriate to think about extending its empire into new fields.'

My own suggestion would be that the criterion of success should be the *ability* of the NEB to sell off these investments at a profit to the tax-payer. Whether they *should* be sold is a political matter, but potential saleability is a purely commercial test. To take an analogy from a different industry : the size of the returns from new roads, if tolls were imposed, is an aid to road investment decisions, even though there may be good (economic as well as political) reasons for not imposing the tolls. Up to the point where congestion occurs, a new motorway has the

[1]'Priorities for the National Enterprise Board', *Financial Times,* 17 February, 1975.

characteristic of a 'public good' (defined p. 64): that its use by one person does not restrict the amount available to another; and charging then results in wasteful under-use. The same argument applies to museum charges on non-crowded days, but such days only: on crowded days use by one more person restricts the space and enjoyment available to others in a museum, so that it is not a public good and pricing is advisable.

An alternative to the NEB

If past experience of such ventures is any guide, the main role of the NEB is likely to be to inject taxpayers' cash into ailing concerns, plus the undertaking of a few regional showpiece projects which have not succeeded in attracting profit-seeking private funds.

There is not the slightest reason to suppose that help for 'lame ducks' or for enterprises of doubtful profitability is a transfer to the poorest members of society. Many people who pay the subsidies in taxes are almost certainly worse off than those who receive the aid.

The one coherent justification for such assistance—and the most generous interpretation of the poll findings—is the desire to cushion people from the effects of change. But in that event the subsidies should be temporary and degressive and not be misrepresented—as the proposals for a National Enterprise Board have been—as a programme for reform and innovation. And it should always be considered whether cash compensation will not give better value to taxpayer and 'lame-duck' employee alike.

Above all, there is the myth that insolvency is the ultimate disaster—which the Labour party prefers to tackle by state ownership and the Conservative by propping up with public funds. No physical assets are destroyed when a concern goes bankrupt, not even the goodwill attaching to component units. The assets are available to new purchasers who see a way of putting them to profitable use.[1] Instead of a National Enterprise Board it would be better to have

(a) a reform of the bankruptcy laws to take some of the sting out of insolvency, without preventing the winding-up of the firms concerned, and

[1] As several entrepreneurs were reported as thinking they could with the bankrupt Aston Martin company.

[29]

(b) an agency to take an active part in breaking-up insolvent concerns into smaller components, with perhaps some public funds to prevent a chain reaction among suppliers and creditors, and to avoid sudden mass dismissals of labour while new owners are being sought. It is absurd to suppose that there is no constructive compromise between indefinite public subvention and instant closures.

Industrial co-operatives

The case against both the indefinite support of 'lame-duck' concerns, and against the view that some central board has a better insight into investment opportunities than decentralised concerns operating in the market, would still be valid if all concerns were state-owned or worker-controlled. Indeed some economists since the 1930s have argued for a system of 'market socialism' which has the advantages of consumer choice and decentralised decisions, without the supposed evils of capitalist ownership.

This claim goes too far for the reasons discussed in Part 2, IV (pp. 87–93) in relation to state socialism. There is, of course, no objection or obstacle to any group setting up a co-operatively-owned enterprise if it can pay its way. The objection to the ventures supported by Mr Anthony Wedgwood Benn is

(a) that they are a reward for the illegal occupation if not seizure of other people's property (known as 'sit-ins'), and

(b) that other taxpayers—*including other workers*—are being coerced through the tax system to subsidise ventures which are believed by Mr Benn's own advisers to have poor prospects of eventually paying their way.

It is no accident that workers' co-operatives have not played a dominating role in any Western economy; and in Yugoslavia, which has tried to establish a system of market socialism based on such enterprises, they have not been an unqualified success. The Yugoslav economy has one of the highest unemployment rates in Europe, and has been a source of migrant labour for many countries further West.

I have nothing to add here to the existing literature on management control and work incentives in such enterprises. But there is a clear-cut technical reason for their disappointing performance. One of the main difficulties of Yugoslav co-operatives is that workers 'can neither sell their rights to future earnings from fixed assets acquired by the firm during their period of employment, nor continue to receive their share of the earnings'.[1] The benefits are therefore limited to the worker's expected period with his firm; and this gives him a strong bias in favour of personal consumption, or individual investment in, for example, savings accounts, one-man businesses, or assets such as jewellery, and against corporate reinvestment. Another difficulty is that

> 'when a firm has invested substantial sums in collective consumption goods, the employees . . . can be expected to resist the hiring of additional workers.'[2]

The lack of incentive to reinvest has driven Yugoslav 'firms' more and more into the hands of the state banks and into 'liquidity crises' of an all too familiar kind. The incentives in the system are in the direction of very high consumption and the finance of capital investment almost exclusively from the banks, which has generated powerful inflationary forces.

The pure labour-managed system has therefore proved unstable. The state had to make a choice: either an extension of property rights to give members of an enterprise a permanent and transferable stake in the capital assets financed through the sacrifice of potential wages, as advocated by some Yugoslav economists; or a move back towards a command economy. The former course was rejected as too much like capitalist equity holding; and the choice in the reforms of 1972 went in favour of more central direction, both of the allocation of co-operative funds between investment and wages, and of the distribution of the wage fund among employees.

Freedom of action has been limited by 'social contracts', but legally enforceable ones in which workers in co-operatives must adjust their aspirations to the 'common good as defined by the industrial group and higher authorities'.[3] This renewed centra-

[1] Eric G. Furbotn and Svetozar Pejovich, 'Property Rights, Economic Decentralisation, and the Evolution of the Yugoslav Firm, 1965–72', *Journal of Law and Economics,* Chicago, October 1973.

[2] The theoretical problems of maintaining full employment in an economy of co-operatives are discussed by Professor J. E. Meade in 'The Theory of Labour-Managed Firms and of Profit Sharing', *Economic Journal,* March 1972, Supplement.

[3] Furbotn and Pejovich, *op. cit.*

lisation has predictably reduced the incentive to efficiency 'since greater earnings yield only modest gains in wages'. There are incentives to falsify information and for managers to seek non-pecuniary incomes in the form of comfort and a quiet life. As with all 'social contracts', substantial resources have to be consumed in monitoring. It is thus less easy to obtain the benefits of a competitive market system while throwing out capitalist ownership than some 'socialists of the chair' would like.

V. 'VOICE' AND 'EXIT'

Voting with one's feet

For all the fuss about 'Bennery' there is remarkably little evidence that most workers do want to run or manage the concerns in which they work. The ORC survey cited (p. 27) asked private sector employees of firms with more than 20 people to indicate the aspirations they considered of most and least importance. 'Workers having seats on boards' was ticked as an important aspiration by 3 per cent. Among aspirations considered of 'least importance', a 'bigger say in management and decision on investment and finance' headed the list, followed by workers having seats on boards. On the other hand, top of the list of most important aspirations was 'more information from the top on what is happening and why'. This finding is merely in accordance with common sense and with most people's personal experience.

Contemporary political and sociological discussion is wrong to assume that the only two choices are obedience to authority and 'democratic' control (i.e. a majority of the activists or articulate who bother to vote), and that the only subject for discussion is the compromise to draw between them in different areas.

A market system provides a third way. An individual can exert his influence by voting with his feet. His most powerful sanction against a tyrannical employer, private or government, or against an unsatisfactory service, is to go elsewhere. His opportunities to vote with his feet are constricted by precisely those elements which it is conventional to praise. First, strong trade unions restrict entry to occupations and prevent people pricing themselves into jobs. Second, 'dashes for growth', financed through the printing press, inevitably end up in more 'stops' and high unemployment that limit choice. Third, state monopoly provision in the social services, which the present Government is trying to extend, limits choice.

A common fallacy is to suppose that the market as an instrument for extending personal choice is of value only to people able to use it—the whole argument about élitism and 'queue jumping' in education and health has been conducted in these terms. As Professor F. A. Hayek has emphasised,

> 'the importance of our being free to do a particular thing has nothing to do with the question of whether we, or the majority, are ever likely to make use of that particular possibility'.[1]

Two highly specific instances of this principle have been given recently by a political scientist in an analysis of the comparative effectiveness of democratic 'voice' and market 'exit'. They show that markets can provide a form of participation superior to anything available from an extension of political processes into every sphere of life.

The first is schools.

> 'Some years ago, my son showed numerous symptoms of anxiety and unhappiness when he moved from nursery school to primary school. It took us a long time to persuade him to say what was wrong, which was that his form teacher bullied and smacked her pupils constantly, for reasons he could not understand. Consultation with neighbours revealed that their children were suffering likewise, but all our off-spring were terrified lest we should complain. As spokesman, I then went to see the headmaster privately, after school hours. He was well aware of the situation but regretted that he could do nothing about it. National Union of Teachers policies made it impossible for teachers to be dismissed, and the Education Authority would not allow headmasters to dump their unsatisfactory teachers on other schools. He saw no alternative to accepting the situation for six years, when the teacher involved would reach retirement age.
>
> 'Three families in my street then transferred their children

[1] *The Constitution of Liberty*, Routledge & Kegan Paul, 1960, Chapter 2, p. 31.

to a private school and accompanied this with a strong letter of protest to the Education Authority. This action apparently had some effect in that a year or so later the teacher retired early. But for the sake of our children none of us would have felt able to protest like this had we not been able to take them elsewhere. In this case exit was the necessary precondition of voice, and the possibility of exit benefited not only our three children but the hundred or so other children who were subsequently able to enjoy their first year in the state primary school without being bullied.'[1]

The second is hospitals :

'Some time ago, I had to have a rather difficult operation on my brain. The surgery was superb, but the nursing care in the neuro-surgical ward left a great deal to be desired. The ward sister suffered from anxiety and migraine; the morale of the nursing staff was extremely low; and this was reflected in treatment that was both inconsiderate and inefficient (in the sense that drugs and medicines were not supplied at the right times). . . .

'My one complaint resulted in such painful retaliation that I decided to keep quiet and conceal the situation from my wife. I changed my mind about this when the patient in the next bed lost his life in rather worrying circumstances . . . When I recounted this story and others to my wife, we decided we would draw on my insurance policies and savings to have me transferred to a private ward, and have my second operation without help from the taxpayer. At the end of the visiting hour my wife . . . intercepted the surgeon in charge of my case in the corridor, demanded an interview and told him what was happening. He was horrified and within an hour a wind of change had blasted through the ward. I will not go into further details, as the general point is clear. *My wife and I could not have taken this action— which benefited all the patients—unless private hospital facilities were available to which I could be transferred. The other patients in the ward knew well enough what was happening, but none of them dared to complain. Here, as*

[1]A. H. Birch, 'Economic Models in Political Science : the Case of "Exit, Voice and Loyalty" ', *British Journal of Political Science,* January 1975.

in the case of the school, exit was not an alternative to voice but a necessary condition for the exercise of voice.' (My italics.)

The implication for policy is clear. The very efficiency of the social services, insofar as they must be provided by government, would be strengthened by the maintenance of a market in education and medical care by enabling, if not positively helping, people to escape from state services through 'exits' to private services. How far exits are best created by tax rebates, grants or perhaps vouchers to consumers who wish to vote with their feet is the interesting subject for discussion, though not on narrowly doctrinal grounds.

VI. NEW THINKING FROM THE NEW WORLD

An impoverished discussion

It is worth at this stage stepping back from specific issues to note some new developments in political economy, which are of far-reaching practical importance but are largely ignored in contemporary British policy discussion to its severe impoverishment. Most of these developments have come from across the Atlantic (often building on foundations laid by Austrian economists such as Schumpeter, von Mises and Hayek, who do not always receive their due acknowledgement). These new approaches are only now beginning to penetrate into the UK, where they are still largely a closed book to many economic practitioners skilled in their own subject and to many students in British universities.

The one trans-Atlantic development that has penetrated British consciousness has the unfortunate label 'monetarism'; and it is largely misunderstood as a technical proposition about banking policy. This leads middle-of-the-road politicians to suppose that the good old British common-sense approach is a little of everything—'a bit of money supply and a bit of incomes policy'.

The real 'monetarist' position is much more disturbing. It is that, contrary to the post-war economic wisdom, the Govern-

[35]

ment does not have the power to fix the level of unemployment by means of 'demand management' of any kind, fiscal or monetary. Attempts to push down the unemployment percentage below a minimum (which can be changed only by fundamental reform of the labour market) leads not merely to inflation, but to runaway inflation and eventual currency collapse, with no permanent benefit to employment.[1]

Five new developments

But the developments in question are far from limited to the inflation-unemployment debate. There are at least five others of outstanding interest for economic analysis and policy.

1. One of the most important for practical affairs is the analysis of markets as a *discovery procedure* in a world where tastes and techniques are changing and information scarce and expensive. This has immediate applications to labour markets and to the analysis of unemployment which are not revealed by the conventional 'demand management' (or 'macro') approach used in the Treasury, taught in British universities, and expounded by many journalists.

2. A second development, outside the monetary sphere, is the analysis of *property rights* and the effects of their different allocations on the use of resources. It is worth emphasising that nearly all the adverse 'externalities', which are so often cited as arguments for non-market decisions, arise from the absence of clearly-defined exclusive property rights or from the transaction costs of certain kinds of contracts. It is because no-one owns the air space, pleasant vistas or the ocean bed that market disciplines do not apply, and exploiters and destroyers can escape without paying a price. If the public authorities do in some sense 'own' the nation's road space, they inflict untold harm by not behaving like owners and instead allowing 'free', and therefore wasteful, use of scarce resources. It is not property rights but their absence which is anti-social. None of this implies, however, that the *existing* distribution of property rights is appropriate—which is a separate question (discussed in pp. 83–87).

3. The third important development relates to the economics of benevolence and charity, which has emphasised the distinc-

[1]This proposition is discussed in my Paper, *Second Thoughts on Full Employment Policy*, Centre for Policy Studies, 1975; and in a rigorous but relatively simple academic exposition by Milton Friedman in IEA Occasional Paper 44, 1975.

tion between *privately chosen* and *selfish* aims. The latter are in no way required for the successful functioning of markets, contrary to popular belief and some of the writings of the early economists.[1]

4. A fourth, and to my mind the most interesting, trend of all has been the development of a political and moral philosophy with the conscious aim of throwing light on questions such as the 'just' distribution of property rights (if there is such a thing), the permissible or required redistribution of income, the legitimacy of the coercion implied by majority voting, and the tax and legislative power of the state.[2]

5. The fifth contribution, of particular relevance to the present *Paper*, is the application of the theory of competition to the political market and to the struggle for votes and powers, as well as to the functions of state bureaucracy. Much British thinking on economic policy is rendered worse than valueless by a sharp contrast between the faults of *real* world markets and the actions of some non-existing and improbable *ideal*, benevolent and omniscient government. Real world markets, with all their faults, have to be compared with real world politicians, civil servants and 'experts'.[3]

Weaknesses of the political market-place

One of the most striking and least controversial results of these studies, and a major obstacle to trendy ideas about referenda and 'participation', is the lack of incentive for the ordinary citizens, and even the minority of active political participants, to become even moderately well informed on major issues. In

[1] A textbook which incorporates the first three developments in comprehensible form is A. A. Alchian and W. R. Allen, *University Economics*, Prentice-Hall International, Paperback Edition, London, 1974. It can be usefully supplemented by A. J. Culyer, *The Economics of Social Policy*, Martin Robertson, 1973. Both contain fallacies (i.e. suggestions or assertions which do not convince me) though they are different from those in the more conventional textbooks, and are also more interesting.

[2] Two contrasting approaches are John Rawls's *A Theory of Justice*, Oxford, 1972, and Robert Nozick, *Anarchy, State and Utopia*, Oxford, 1974. A new contribution still to be assessed is James Buchanan, *The Limits of Liberty*, Chicago, 1975.

[3] A restatement of the political economy of politics, sometimes known as 'public choice' theory, is in the Hobart Paper, *The Economics of Politics*, by Professor Gordon Tullock (1975). The Hobart Paperback (No. 5) by Professor W. A. Niskanen applies aspects of the theory to bureaucracies. The economics of politics is regularly discussed in *Public Choice*, the organ of the Center for Study of Public Choice, Virginia Polytechnic Institute and State University, Blacksburg, Virginia.

private lives, the cash constraint is an influence for rationality. People know in household budgeting that more of one thing means less of something else. They know they can improve the trade-offs, for example, between leisure and take-home pay, by a careful choice of where to live; but they know that such improvements are not unlimited and themselves cost effort to find. By contrast, the constraint of national resources is too abstract and remote for the same persons to take on board as voters. The Opposition politician has no interest in explaining it, while Ministers must at least compete on promises of future performance. There is thus an endemic tendency to over-estimate what governments can achieve and an ever-present danger of trying to satisfy simultaneously incompatible demands by the use of the monetary printing press (for which all too many economists are all too willing to find a rationalisation).[1]

A further set of complications arises from the incentives within the bureaucratic process. The chain which links voters' preferences with the day-to-day behaviour of the individual official is long, and it has many weak links. On the other hand, close connections inevitably develop between the regulating agency and those whom it is supposed to regulate—whether it is the Department of Education and the teachers or the Bank of England and the City.

Even if voters' views were well-considered and could be translated into action with perfect efficiency by the government machine, there would be a prior difficulty in defining what we mean by 'the majority view'. This is an ambiguous concept if there are more than two alternative policies. It is well known that the decision taken by a committee can depend on the accident of the order in which amendments are considered.[2] These difficulties are enormously compounded by the complex policy bundles between which voters are supposed to choose at elections (of course, they do no such thing).

---

[1]This theme is developed in my article, 'The Economic Contradictions of Democracy', *British Journal of Political Science,* April 1975.

[2]The best chance of securing a clear-cut result would be to have a series of votes on all possible alternatives considered in pairs. Even then a cyclical result—B is preferred to A, C is preferred to B, but A is preferred to C—cannot be ruled out. It is indeed quite likely on issues involving many voters and a variety of possible actions. A comprehensible summary of these aspects of voting theory can be found in Appendix 2 of Buchanan and Tullock, *The Calculus of Consent,* University of Michigan Press, Ann Arbor, 1962 (second edn., 1965).

VII. OLD THINKING FROM THE OLD WORLD

Pressure group influences

There are many other defects of the political market. There is the possible oppression of a minority by a bare majority, or of the majority by a coalition of minorities with strong views on particular issues. Special interest groups are likely to prevail over more general interests, because of the concentration of the former and the dispersion of the latter. The beneficial impact of any one protectionist or restrictionist measure on an individual via his professional or geographical interest is far stronger than any loss he may bear along with 50 or 60 million other citizens.

Advocates of the 'Corporate State', or of concordats between the Government, TUC and CBI, make the mistake of assuming that, if there is a fair balance between business and labour interests, and between different regions and industries, all will be well. Indeed they regard the clash of interest groups as itself part of the working of the beneficent invisible hand.

The fundamental weakness of this position has been exposed by Professor Mancur Olson :

'Even if a pressure group system worked with perfect *fairness* for every group, it would still tend to work *inefficiently*. If every industry is favoured, to a fair or equal degree, by favourable government policies obtained through lobbying, the economy as a whole will tend to function less efficiently, and every group will be worse off than if none, or only some, of the special interest demands had been granted. Coherent, rational policies cannot be expected from a series of *ad hoc* concessions to diverse interest groups.'[1]

'Consumerism'

Pressure group politics are often identified with producer groups, whether business or trade union, or the two combined. There can, however, also be consumer interest groups, with equally deleterious effects.

The pressure for cheap mortgages is a demand by one group

[1]Mancur Olson, Jr., *The Logic of Collective Action: Public Goods and the Theory of Groups,* Harvard University Press, Cambridge, Mass., 1965 (2nd edn., 1971), p. 124.

of taxpayers for a subsidy from the rest of the community. This is over and above the tax privileges they already receive.[1] The case to be made in their favour is at most second best. Some offset is necessary to the large subsidies on rented council houses, if there is not to be an artificial deterrent to home ownership. A true comparison is made extremely difficult because of permanent 'shortages' of council dwellings and the consequential waiting lists.

Generally speaking, pressure for below-market prices for any product is the expression of some consumer interest group, with no *prima facie* claim to more attention than comparable producer pressures. One insidious kind of 'consumerism' consists in lobbying producers or legislators to insist on standards or specifications which individual consumers do not desire— either because they do not think the changes worth the money or because they positively dislike them. This has reached its apogee in the American cars which emit a piercing scream and refuse to start if the safety belt is left unfastened. The dividing line between insisting on information for transmission to customers, and forcing some people's values and tastes down the throats of others, is a very tricky one, which consumer bodies are always in danger of crossing.

Then again, the supposed interest of consumers in lower prices is deceptive, if they are imposed at the expense of quality, availability, or future supplies. There is all the difference in the world between promoting competition by uncovering collusion, and attempting to roll back the share of profits or make a stand against inflation. Cutting competitive margins and resisting inflation are beyond the power and the competence of 'consumer bodies'; and if they have any influence in these directions it will be to endanger future investment and employment and—paradoxically—to promote a pattern of resource allocation different from that desired by consumers themselves, as shown in their market-place behaviour.

[1]The main privilege is not, as is so often assumed, the tax exemption (up to a limit) of interest payments. It is the abolition of Schedule A—the former tax on the notional rental value of a house. That this is a privilege can be seen by considering the deterioration in the tax position of a householder if he sells his house and puts an equivalent capital sum into marketable securities. House and security prices should move in such a way as to offset the disadvantages of such an exchange at the margin. But the artificial incentive to own houses rather than other forms of property remains.

VIII. NEW MARKETS TO SOLVE NEW PROBLEMS

Conventional interventionism

The text that follows (Part 2) is taken with minor alterations from my *Capitalism and the Permissive Society,* with an insertion from a smaller volume, *Is There an Economic Consensus?*[1] The *Capitalism* book was avowedly a work in political economy, not in a partisan sense, but in its emphasis on the links between personal, political and economic freedom and the rule of law; and in its argument that *competitive* capitalism was most likely to minimise the role of authority and give people the most opportunity 'to do their own thing'.

The emphasis of the extracts in Part 2 is different. In developing my argument, I had to say a good deal about the role and logic of markets and prices in any kind of society, and from the point of view of widely differing value-judgements. The IEA kindly offered to publish some of these passages dealing with the nature of markets *per se.* Naturally, I hope that these extracts will tempt people to read the original books.

Like many IEA *Papers,* the present one is addressed both to people actively engaged in public affairs who want an insight into economic thinking, and to students. The latter will not need to be told that it should be regarded as a supplement to, rather than as a substitute for, normal textbooks. If I have given some idea of what is, or could be, the value of supply and demand analysis, and its more unexpected implications the purpose will have been served.

The new developments in political economy mentioned on pp. 35–39 have helped to reinforce my views on the role of markets. But I came to these conclusions by a more personal route—from my more casual observations as an economic journalist, which made me feel there was something seriously deficient in the British academic economic tradition as well as in the Eastern seaboard US texts favoured in this country. Above all I was profoundly dissatisfied both with the conventional interventionist case, which was based on lapses from 'perfection' in the workings of markets, and with the textbook case for free enterprise, which described the optimum allocation of resources with known and static tastes and techniques.

[1] Both published by Macmillan in 1973.

In Part 2 there is also some analysis of the effects of different policies on personal freedom as well as on economic efficiency. The former is just as much amenable to dispassionate study as the latter. Indeed 'efficiency' is at least as difficult and as problematic a concept as 'freedom', and effects on the two values are much more difficult to disentangle than is generally realised.

Section VI of Part 2 is concerned with a specific problem : the role of markets and prices in a 'less materialist society'; and it offers some practical proposals. The economic problem is never likely to be banished so long as scarcities of some kind remain—and this is likely to be for ever if we think of scarcity of space, time, of interesting work, even without venturing into such intangibles as status, affection or self-esteem. But society can become less materialistic, in the sense that additions to take-home pay could come to seem of minor importance to most individuals, compared with increases in leisure or in job interest, in congenial working conditions or in improved human relations. Such a change could come about either from the side of tastes or because the increase in material production had reached a point where further increases were of diminished importance.

The premature end of growth

It may seem utopian to consider such possibilities at a time when all the talk is of the inevitability of reduced living standards owing to the impact of higher oil prices on the industrial world in general and the UK in particular. Nevertheless, I think that the fashionable reaction against growth has been overdone. The once-for-all reduction in 1974 consumption levels required for a sustainable UK overseas balance of payments varies between nil and 8 per cent, to cover the extreme range of the optimists and the pessimists.[1] From then on there is no reason why growth of consumption as well as production should not be resumed, unless incentives are blunted even more than in the past by policies based on envy, irrationality or short-sighted political expediency. These are policies we are free not to follow.

Nor is the so-called energy crisis, or the case for recycling waste products, a reason to put a brake on growth. Keynes once remarked that 'a certain hoarding instinct, a readiness

[1]*Crisis '75 . . ?, op. cit.*

to be alarmed and excited by the idea of exhaustion of resources' was a common psychological trait. He was referring to
Stanley Jevons's alarm a hundred years ago about the exhaustion of British coal stocks.[1] So far in human history, rising relative prices of energy, raw materials or whatever else has been
causing alarm, have elicited new supplies or the production of
substitutes. If the new supplies or substitutes are not available,
rising relative prices will themselves act as a brake on material
growth without any dramatic 'zero growth' policies.

Much the greater likelihood is of resumed growth in countries
where the price mechanism and decentralised initiative are allowed to operate (as they are to some extent even in Communist
countries despite the difficulties discussed in pp. 87–93). More attention will, one hopes, be paid to reducing the 'bads' that come
with the increased goods, such as pollution, transport congestion, increased travelling time, destruction of visual amenities
or of the architectural heritage. If these improvements are not
reflected in Gross Domestic Product (GDP) figures, this failure
is a defect in the statistics and not a true slowing down in the
growth rate.

Inflation—the less obvious effects

Rapid and uncertain rates of inflation, well into double digit
percentages, are at one and the same time the biggest obstacle to
the effective functioning of markets and the biggest influence for
the perpetration of petty materialist and mercenary attitudes.
There is no paradox. When markets are prevented from carrying out their signalling role efficiently, we have to pay far
closer and more obsessive attention to them than normally.
When the general price level is stable, the absolute changes required in particular prices to enable the market to do its jobs
are modest enough not to raise an outcry; but during a rapid
inflation the absolute changes are obtrusive and the volume of
opposition mounts.

It is easy to see why. Let us suppose that fares have to go
up by 5 per cent in relation to other prices, while clothes can go
down by 5 per cent. If these changes are superimposed on a
25 per cent inflation, fares have to rise by 31 per cent and

[1][Extracts from Jevons's *The Coal Question* will be found in Colin
Robinson, *The Energy 'Crisis' and British Coal*, Hobart Paper 59, IEA,
1974.—ED.]

[43]

clothes themselves *rise* by 19 per cent. There is likely to be opposition even to the change in clothes prices—which is in truth a (relative) *reduction*; and the 31 per cent increase in fares will give rise to opposition and protest action. The news media are full of reports about 'rising prices', many of them saying no more than that products have gone up in cost in line with the rate of inflation—reports which would have been non-stories with a stable general price level. Thus one of the worst effects of inflation is to make us more grasping, mean-spirited and mercenary than under stable prices.

Selective perception works with a vengeance. People are more conscious of the prices that have risen by more than the prevailing inflation rate than of those that have risen by less. And they are more conscious of the rise in all prices than in wages. We can therefore expect pressure for both price controls and for subsidies, often in an opposite direction to that which would be required to improve the market mechanism.

If the rate of inflation is 20 per cent, a person paying £500 per annum in a controlled tenancy would have his payment raised to £600 if he is to pay the same *real* rent as before. A rise of this magnitude provokes enough protest. The hope of going any further and gradually narrowing the gap between controlled and market rent would be regarded as 'politically impossible'. The gap tends instead to widen as a result of partial or complete rent freezes imposed for electoral expediency, such as that of 1974–75. In Germany in October 1922, well before the inflation had reached its final hysterical phase, prices in general were 400 times what they were before the war, but rents were only 10 times as high. In terms of currency of constant purchasing power, this meant that a tenant who paid 100 marks in 1914 was paying a mere $2\frac{1}{2}$ marks in 1922. It is likely that many British council house tenants are paying derisorily low (real) rents in 1975, particularly as a proportion of their increasing household incomes.

Indexation—second best, but vital

It is too defeatist to call for an end to inflation and to leave it at that. The difficulties—whether 'political' or 'economic'—in the way of ending inflation quickly do not excuse us from looking for second-best solutions if we are to prevent the drift of the UK into the state of Albania in a bad year. The restoration of the price mechanism as a method of transmitting information and allocating resources can begin right now. The first essential is to replace the pound with something else as a *standard of value*. Contracts can be made in terms of any price index, or a hard currency such as the mark, or in gold units. There is nothing in English law to prevent such contracts being enforced, provided the sums of money eventually paid are sterling, and the contract specifies exactly by what index the sterling sum has to be multiplied.

One of the biggest impediments to the working of markets is that each forward-looking transaction has to face two kinds of uncertainty: those normal to the particular product and service, and an extra gamble on the rate of inflation. The second uncertainty could be much reduced by indexed (or 'constant purchasing power') contracts. The subject of indexation requires a work to itself (and many are being written). But we should distinguish between the inflation-proofing of the tax system, which depends on government action, and private contracts, which are up to the individuals concerned.[1]

If fears of the attitude of the Price Commission are the obstacle, it should be remembered that the present price control legislation, which was imposed by a Conservative Government, runs out early in 1976. The Price Code would have broken down long ago without a degree of 'goodwill' which it did not deserve. There is still everything to play for in the new legislation. Some Labour Ministers are themselves looking for an excuse to withdraw from a system of regulation of Byzantine complexity; and we would never have reached the present situation had not the organised representatives of British industry co-operated with (and even initiated, as in the 'voluntary' price restraint of 1971) measures thoroughly inimical to the workings of a market system, but with zero or even adverse impact on the rate of inflation.

[1]'Constant purchasing power' contracts are most difficult in the capital market. If interest payments are augmented to compensate for inflation, the supplements are taxed as if real income has increased. Alternatively, if the principal is inflation-proofed, the repayment ranks as a capital gain. In addition, there is the 'discouragement' of such bonds by the Treasury and Bank of England. Although a reform of the tax law here is a matter of urgency, there is some degree of risk which would make it worthwhile to issue indexed bonds even under present rules.

IX. POINTERS FOR POLICY

The aim of this introductory Part has not been to outline a detailed programme, but to show the topical importance of the market as a way of giving more power to the people over their own lives, superior to state-enforced 'participation' by unions and other collective bodies. But a resumé of a few of the policy pointers might be found helpful.

1. Welfare and poverty

Consumer choice is as important for services such as housing, health and education as it is for over-the-counter purchases. The first essential is to protect existing avenues of choice against attempts to confine everyone to state services. Subsidies, rationing and controls of 'essentials' (whether foodstuffs or imports) are not only wasteful and anti-libertarian, but are also a very inefficient method of helping poorer people. A good deal could, however, be done to mitigate the evils of existing policies by making rights to council houses, coupons, quotas, etc. (if forced upon us) transferable in the market.

2. Industry

In industrial policy, the role of bodies such as the NEB should be to provide temporary help for the victims of change and to bring existing state investments to a level of efficiency at which they *could* be sold at a profit to the taxpayer.

3. Inflation and trade unions

The two great obstacles to the effective functioning of markets are (a) inflation and (b) the behaviour of coercive monopolistic groups, of which the unions are now the most important. It is unlikely that an overnight solution will be found to either problem; but the beginning of wisdom is to realise that 'Keynesian' demand management has run its course and is now an engine for producing both more inflation and more unemployment, and that inflation is the biggest single force increasing union power.

4. Indexation

Until such time as political credibility can be accorded to a government undertaking to control monetary demand over the long haul, the 'indexation' of contracts is a vital second best if civilised economic life is to continue.

[46]

5. *The state or voluntary co-operation?*

But ultimately the reforms most needed are in the political market-place to prevent the oppression of both minorities and majorities and the whipping up of unrealistic expectations about what can be achieved by state or collective action, as distinct from what people can achieve for themselves through their individual behaviour or by voluntary co-operation.[1]

---

[1] Some very tentative brief suggestions are in my contribution to *Crisis '75..?*, Occasional Paper Special (43), IEA, January 1975.

PART 2

Principles of the Market

I. THE MARKET IN THEORY

Judging the market economy

How can the market operate so that individuals pursuing their own self-chosen (not necessarily selfish) interests also promote the general well-being and refrain from hampering it? The following three italicised propositions represent the point of view that seemed to me to emerge from an examination of 'objective multiple choice' questions and 'approved' (i.e. 'correct') answers in elementary tests administered to students. A recent survey among economists suggested that the 'mainstream' outlook given below would be shared by over 75 per cent, although some with qualifications.[1] It will therefore do as a starting point, even though my own emphasis would differ on a number of aspects.

1. Competitive markets and the pursuit by individuals of their own interests can—with definable exceptions—produce an effective and prosperous economic system, and a reasonable harmony between public and private interest. Although such a harmony can be provided by a competitive capitalist system, the key to success is not ownership, but freely operating competitive markets, which can also be envisaged in a socialist economy where enterprises are state-owned.

2. Free markets will not necessarily bring about a desirable distribution of income (a matter of personal judgement). But the way to improve distribution is by direct cash grants and taxes, or improvement of opportunities, rather than by interfering in the market-place.

3. Such interference can sometimes be justified, for a totally different purpose. The market works effectively only if enterprises and individuals pay for all the costs that their activities impose on the rest of the community and if a price is charged for all benefits conferred. Where there are costs, such as pollution by automobile exhaust or factory waste products, for which those responsible do not pay, or where benefits are conferred for which it is impracticable to make individual charges, state interference is necessary. But it is best achieved by adjusting relative prices

[1]Details of the questionnaire and survey are in my *Is There an Economic Consensus?*, Macmillan, 1973. On housing nearly half had (in my view unconvincing) qualms about applying the market approach.

*through taxes and subsidies—and on occasion by the state provision
of services—rather than by direct controls or prohibitions.*

Subscribers to this outlook would accept that considerable unemployment can exist because of the slowness of wages and prices
to respond to changing supply and demand conditions. They
disagree among themselves about how far the unemployment can
be mitigated through 'demand management', i.e. budgetary policy
and control over the creation of money. Many would now
argue that more fundamental remedies are required, e.g. to make
it more difficult for unions to use their monopoly power to price
members out of jobs, or to make mobility—at present impeded by
rent controls—easier and break down artificial job demarcations.

The history of economics is largely that of a running debate
between the mainstream economic orthodoxy and its critics, whose
characteristic achievements have been to point out the weaknesses
of that orthodoxy (which is perhaps now more convincingly form-
ulated as a result) rather than to outline a convincing alternative.

It so happens that I have some sympathy with the participants
in the survey who protested against the undefined use of the term
'efficiency' and I would prefer to analyse the merits of a market
economy in somewhat different terms, openly emphasising its de-
pendence on certain value-judgements, political probabilities and
impressionistic empirical generalisations.

Opinion among economists

Whether or not an economist was prepared to subscribe to the
market orthodoxy often depended on whether he was prepared to
treat questions of the allocation of resources on their own merits, in
the belief that any major undesired effect on the distribution of
income could be offset, or more than offset, by the tax and social
security system (as well as by more fundamental policies designed
to improve educational opportunities and remove monopolistic restrictions on entry into occupations). The view of the minority of
dissentient economists was that it was impossible to make any
judgement about any aspect of the allocation of resources or of
economic organisation without taking specific account of distribution. There were genuine fears that orthodox measures for improving allocation or increasing consumer choice would have important
distributional effects, which might not tend to cancel out, but could
well be adverse and outweigh the other benefits claimed for
them. A recent topical example was whether it was possible to
compensate for the adverse effect of higher food and fuel prices by
a sufficient adjustment of pensions, family allowances and the tax
starting point.

The fatal flaw in the economic outlook of the critics of the 'New Left'[1] is the belief that one does not have to choose between a market and a command economy or between varying mixtures of the two; and that there is a third ethically preferable system which would rely on more spontaneous and less selfish motives. A large part of Professor Assar Lindbeck's *The Political Economy of the New Left*[2] is taken up with a sympathetic but relentless analysis of this fallacy.

Lindbeck conveniently summarises the five standard problems of any society which have caused generations of economists to doubt that one can have an economy dispensing with both markets and bureaucratic commands. These are the needs :

(1) to obtain *information* about people's preferences;

(2) to *allocate* men, machines, land, buildings and other resources in accordance with these preferences;

(3) to *decide* which production techniques to use;

(4) to create *incentives* to avoid unnecessarily costly methods, to invest, to develop new technologies and products; and

(5) (and perhaps most important) to *co-ordinate* the desires of millions of individuals, firms and households.

This list is provided not by Professor Milton Friedman or Professor F. A. Hayek, but by a Swedish Social Democrat whose book is offered as an antidote to them. I would only add that four at least of these requirements do not depend on selfishness but on the need for co-ordinating and signalling devices which would still exist even if we could rely more on people's goodwill. Remarks such as Adam Smith's about addressing ourselves not to the 'humanity' but to the 'self-love' of others and Alfred Marshall's about men's motives 'in the ordinary business of life' give a misleading impression. Even if people were actuated by benevolence, they would still need to know *which* jobs to do and *which* methods to use to satisfy other people's desires most efficiently, and a co-ordinating mechanism would be required. At most we could dispense with the fourth item on the list—incentives. Even then the profits or opportunities for high earnings would still be indispensable as *signals*, although any excess wealth gained by following them might eventually be given away to others.

---

[1]The term 'New Left' is used for people who are against the 'system' they believe to be capitalist, but have lost the faith of the Old Left in state socialism, and insist on the individual's right to his own life-style.

[2]Harper & Row, 1971.

Professor J. K. Galbraith's influence has, as Lindbeck has pointed out, strengthened the temptation to ignore the inconvenient problem of co-ordination. Galbraith fails to explain how the few large firms on which he concentrates—let alone millions of householders and individuals—co-ordinate their activities. He concentrates on planning *within* firms, and many readers overlook that he has said nothing about relations *between* firms, except by quasi-mystical references to the 'technostructure'.[1]

Can computers replace the market?

Lindbeck also lays to rest the illusion that computers could take over from markets the functions listed. Complicated messages about preferences, product qualities and information on production processes cannot be coded on to a computer. This is more than a practical impossibility. Even if consumers could *immediately* translate into computer language their preferences between an indefinitely large set of alternatives made possible by technology, they do not themselves know how they would react to *new* kinds of goods or changes in quality or innovation in general, for the simple reason that people do not always know how they themselves will react in *hypothetical* circumstances. Even when it comes to communicating details of production processes it is difficult to envisage how the specifics of 'knowing how' could be put into a computer. Moreover, all this effort, even if successful, would simply reproduce the data already presented by prices, profits and sales figures.

Does the market fabricate wants?

A dominant feature of fashionable thinking, again powerfully stimulated by Galbraith, is a denial that the market does allow people to 'do their own thing'. Consumer wants, it is alleged, are artificially fabricated by advertising and other sales techniques. The art of salesmanship has never been regarded as quite respectable. It has, of course, always been disliked by conservative traditionalists, and strictures here are no monopoly of the New Left. Dr E. J. Mishan has argued strongly against advertising from the premises of conventional economic theory; and Mr Charles Carter, the Secretary General of the Royal Economic Society and notable university administrator, has outlined a complex scheme excluding from tax-deductible expenses most marketing expenditure, including sales staff and packaging, as well as promotion and advertising, and imposing a prohibitive tax on such expenditure when it exceeds a certain proportion of turnover.[2]

[1] J. K. Galbraith, *The New Industrial State,* Penguin Books, 1969.
[2] Charles Carter, *Wealth,* Penguin Books, 1971, pp. 136 *et seq.*

Such writers do not, however, go to the lengths of asserting that firms can create a demand for whatever goods they choose to produce. As Lindbeck has pointed out, the latter is a new form of 'Say's Law'—so much attacked by Keynes for giving too *favourable* an impression of the capitalist system—which asserted that supply created its own demand and which thereby denied the possibility of a depression. The new form of the law seeems to assert that this is true not merely for the economy as a whole but for each individual firm or product.

The belief is quite false. Simply because firms do not limit themselves to supplying demands felt by the human race when it left the Garden of Eden, but actively build up a market for their products, this does not mean they can impose whatever they like on a defenceless public. The British motor industry has not been able to prevent consumers from buying more imported cars; Cunard has been unable to prevent a fall in demand for passenger shipping lines; the Coal Board was unable to prevent a switch to other fuels; and there are countless other examples.[1] Marketing studies suggest that among products regarded as 'technical successes' only perhaps 10–20 per cent survive market and pre-launching studies, while of those that are launched one-third to one-half are withdrawn as failures within one year.[2]

There are two extreme and equally absurd prevalent models of the role of the consumer. There is, on the one hand, the view that people have innate tastes which firms exist to satisfy. Hardly any reputable economist, however orthodox, has ever explicitly held this view; but there are incautious statements, particularly in American textbooks, which give credence to this allegation of Galbraith's.[3] At the other extreme is the view, to which Galbraith himself comes perilously close, that sees consumers as plastic clay on which the advertisers can impose any shape they like. In practice, salesmanship is part of the process of widening the range of alternatives of which people are aware. Like many other technological and cultural techniques, it develops desires of which people were not aware before and – the point must be conceded— causes some people to be more dissatisfied with their lot than they otherwise would be. This is part of the price of freedom of communication. Nearly all the products of civilisation—arts, sports and

[1] For details of these and many other instances, Professor Frank McFadzean, *Galbraith and the Planners,* University of Strathclyde, 1968, and Professor G. C. Allen, *Economic Fact and Fantasy,* Occasional Paper No. 14, IEA, 2nd edn., 1969.

[2] Lindbeck, *op. cit.,* p. 43.

[3] Cited in Galbraith, *Economics, Peace and Laughter,* André Deutsch, 1971, p. 72.

recreations, just as much as running water, telephones or labour-saving gadgets—have been invented and sold to people who were not spontaneously asking for any of them, but were glad to have them when they arrived. It is part of the function of a market economy to suggest new possibilities to people which they are then free to accept or reject. It may be that commercial advertising increases demand for consumer goods relative to 'public goods', leisure or a pleasant environment. But politicians, writers and journalists can and do propagandise in the opposite direction.[1]

None of this means that the situation in advertising or consumer information is incapable of reform. If advertisers really discovered and used forms of subliminal advertising, which exercised a literally hypnotic effect that people were powerless to resist, the case for legal prohibition of these forms would be strong. Much more could moreover be done to encourage the provision of information and views on products from points of view other than the producer's. The case for state encouragement and financial support of consumer bodies is that it is still too difficult to organise or finance anything analogous to the political 'Opposition' in the commercial sphere.

Choice—a burden to be delegated?

Another objection to markets is that the exercise of choice itself involves costs and inconvenience which some people do not wish to bear. In many aspects of life an attempt to survey the total range of options would be impracticable, because the consumer lacks the knowledge to make it, or irrational, because the benefits are too trivial in relation to the time and effort expended; and there may be advantages in voluntarily delegating the choice to others. Investment and unit trusts spare the investor the bother of selecting his securities; organisations such as the AA and *The Good Food Guide* select hotels and restaurants and group them into convenient grades. Travel agents offer both package and individual tours for people who cannot be bothered to make their own arrangements. There are excellent 'flower clubs' which, for a fixed annual subscription, arrange a weekly delivery of the flowers that supply the best value for money at the time of year. This gives access to both expertise and to economies of bulk purchasing beyond most individuals acting on their own. Every encouragement should be given to such methods of delegating choice; and we can all exercise our own preferences about which purchases to delegate, and to whom.

[1]The activities of the New Left are themselves part of the free market in ideas, and by no means the least successful part of it.

It is true that we still have to choose between investment trusts, or between advisers on investment trusts, between hotel guides, and so on. A resurrected and expanded Consumer Council or similar body could publish lists of organisations fulfilling minimum standards. The appropriateness of the standards and their application to particular instances will always be open to argument and there will be nothing sacrosanct about the lists; but they would, at least, provide reassurance to people instinctively afraid of being cheated by commercial enterprises. In the social service area, no one need be forced to 'shop around' for private education and health services, however much such private provision is encouraged, so long as state services of the present standard or higher continue to exist side by side.

Poverty and equality

Another common objection to competitive markets reflects a renewed outburst of egalitarian sentiment. It is certainly possible to go a long way towards 'levelling up' the conditions of the poorest section of the population under capitalism. A well-founded criticism of modern industrial society, which applies to both the 'capitalist' and the Communist countries, is the amount of poverty that continues despite average levels of real income per head which are very high by all past standards. Poverty usually means an income below that required to maintain an 'adequate' standard of living for the family or individual. Although the notion of an 'adequate' standard rises with average income levels, it is not meaningless to speak of a whole society being poor—for example, when the *average* standard of living, however defined, is insufficient to prevent starvation or gross malnutrition. But as society becomes richer, it becomes more and more reasonable to regard the poor as those with less than some given minimum proportion of average post-tax real income (adjusted for family size and other complications). The size of this minimum is necessarily arbitrary. But it is perfectly possible to set up as a goal that no household of average size should have an income of less than, say, a third of the national average.[1] By guaranteeing an income of this kind, there is a limited sense in which the poor need not always be with us. Poverty is

[1]The best available estimate for 1972 is that there were 17 million households with, on average, disposable incomes approaching £2,600. The proposed minimum would then be nearly £900—more for families with several children, less for smaller households. (For comparison, the supplementary benefit rates amounted to nearly £660 for a married couple plus about £100–£150 per child according to age.) This figure will rise in future years both with real income and inflation.

partly an absolute and partly a relative phenomenon. A family which earns a given and small proportion of the national average is not poor in the same sense, when this involves having only one car and having to share a swimming pool, as when it involves infants dying of starvation.

A guaranteed income could be provided at first in the form of a negative income tax, but eventually distributed as a social dividend to all, whether at work or not.[1] It is a way in which those who did not wish to participate in a consumption-oriented, work-obsessed society could 'opt out' of it, without imposing an unwanted revolution on the rest of the population. The main object of such a scheme would, however, be to provide guarantees against extreme poverty for everyone. Yet we would be wise not to expect too much from it, especially in the early years. As Professor Harry Johnson has pointed out,[2] there are limits to the degree of earnings transfer, whether in guaranteed incomes or other forms that the bulk of the population will tolerate. Moreover, many poor people do not share the anti-consumption ethos and would be glad of the opportunity to earn more than any feasible income guarantee is likely to provide.

The most promising, although most difficult, way of helping such people is to increase their opportunity to acquire the skills demanded in the market place. Lack of knowledge of technical trends and opportunities leads children to follow their parents' occupation into what Professor Johnson has called 'perpetual pockets of poverty'. While the provision of 'free' or subsidised information or training would help, the inclination of those who are hostile to market forces is to conserve the population of existing districts and industries by a variety of make-work devices, which hinder the geographical and occupational mobility that would, in the long run, provide the victims of change with their best opportunities.

Discrimination and poverty

Many kinds of discrimination make for poverty. Racial discrimination is a less important factor in Britain than in the USA, but there is plenty of discrimination against the old, by compulsory retiring ages, against women by exclusion from work they could perform, such as compositing, and against the young, by forcing children to stay on at school for longer and longer periods. It is worth noting that the more profit-seeking and less bureaucratic a

[1]Discussed further, pp. 111–113.
[2]In *The Economic Approach to Social Questions,* Weidenfeld & Nicolson, 1968.

firm, and the less hamstrung it is by unions or staff associations, the more incentive it will have to provide work for elderly people who may not be worth a normal wage but who may still be able to render some productive service.

Apart from their macro-economic effects, trade union monopolies—by raising relative wages in a few supposedly skilled or semi-skilled trades, such as the motor industry or printing—reduce the welfare of other workers. Trade unions on both sides of the Atlantic have also raised unemployment by insisting on above-market wage-rates and/or minimum wage laws for the less skilled occupations. Those particularly hard hit have been the untrained, or less easily employable, not least, women, the young and the disabled, who could have found a niche at wages corresponding to their productivity, but have now been pushed out of the labour market and onto relief, to the applause of bogus humanitarians.

To many critics, however, egalitarianism involves not only a 'levelling up' in the conditions of the poor, but also an elimination of all major disparities of income so that no one is much above some general average. It is certainly possible to modify the distribution of income and wealth without destroying a market economy, if appropriate methods of redistribution are used. But there are limits to the process. Despite the achievements of capitalism in breaking down class barriers, any viable capitalist system does involve the existence of individuals many times wealthier than average. The same applies to non-capitalist economies where market forces are allowed a role. This can be seen, for example, in the tendency in some Eastern European countries to pay bonuses out of profits to managers of state undertakings, which has obvious analogies to capitalist practices.

If all material differentials are intolerable, *the only alternative is centralised direction of labour.* This is the lesson of Western economic theory and Communist economic practice. There comes a point at which radicals of all hues have to choose between their commitment to freedom of choice of occupation and life-style, and extreme egalitarianism. With those to whom equality of material reward is the one absolute value to which everything else must be subordinated, no further argument is possible. But I doubt very much if this is the ultimate position of most of today's young radicals. If they could understand that the single-minded pursuit of equality would lead to the sacrifice of other valued goals, most of them would probably modify their attitude. Too much New Left writing seems to assume that the wealth of some individuals is *necessarily* the *cause* of the poverty of others. As Professor Lindbeck has put it, economic activity is seen as a 'zero-sum' game, where what is gained by one person is lost by another. This ties in all too well with the distaste for patient analysis which is one of the less attractive features of fashionable thinking.

Pressure groups and government

There is a much better case against the concentration of power in the hands of what President Eisenhower dramatised as the 'military-industrial complex', or the scandalous ability of interest and pressure groups of all kinds to obtain special favours, ranging from import controls to tax exemptions, tariffs and subsidies. Although these influences may be especially noticeable in the USA, they are not absent in Britain. Tempting though it may be to quote the stock example of the special tax depletion allowances, production controls and import quotas for American oil producers, I am not persuaded that tax privileges for British home owners —which redistribute income from the poor to the better off—are on an altogether higher plane of virtue.

Many of these abuses are the result of the *absence* of competitive market pressures, not their presence; and this is, in turn, due in most cases to extensive paternalistic intervention of the kind for so long preached by people in all three British political parties. It is too easy to persuade politicians and officials whose own money is not at stake that journeys to the moon, ever more advanced aircraft, or home-based computer industries, should be subsidised from the public purse. Governments find it notoriously difficult to separate genuine defence needs from the inevitable desire of the 'military-industrial complex' for elaborate, ever more expensive forms of hardware. It is not an accident that the danger of Galbraith's 'New Industrial State' is most precisely where government involvement with business is closest and most specific. Professor Galbraith is so intent on ridiculing market-oriented economists (for the benefit of a mass readership that will accept on trust his account of their views) that he accepts a quite unnecessarily fatalistic attitude to the trends about which he is supposed to be worrying, and dismisses all remedies that do not involve ever more frequent and personalised involvement between government and business.[1]

The remedy for these evils lies in the direction of more competition, more reliance on markets and more reliance on the price mechanism, adjusted to take into account 'social' costs and benefits at present unpriced. It does not lie in the suppression of 'capitalism' and even more concentration of power at the centre. To

[1] For one of many instances, Galbraith, *The American Left and Some British Comparisons,* Fabian Tract No. 406, 1971.

[60]

cite Lindbeck yet again : would Concorde be less likely to have been built if the British and French Governments not only co-operated with the aircraft producers but also entirely owned them (as they partially do already)? The valid elements in the objection to the cult of technology and growth of measurable GNP arise from the intervention of governments to impose on the community more hardware of every sort, whether computers, satellite systems or common-or-garden machinery benefiting from 'investment incentives', than would be provided if firms interested in these areas had to compete unaided for the customer's or saver's purse.

II. USES AND ABUSES OF THE MARKET ECONOMY

A number of overlapping, but far from identical, terms have been used to label an economic system characterised by markets, decentralised decisions and a wide range of choices for consumer and producer. They include *the market economy, the price mechanism, competition, the profit motive, capitalism, private enterprise* and *a free economy,* to name only a few. They differ considerably in the political direction of their sales appeal.

Market economy, price mechanism, capitalism

'The market economy' and 'the price mechanism' are, in concept at least, independent of the structure of ownership; and they do not involve a commitment to the capitalist system. Some would argue that competition and even a form of the profit motive could be combined with state- or syndicalist-ownership, as is attempted for example in Yugoslavia. 'Capitalism', of course, indicates the private ownership of the means of production, distribution and exchange; but it will also be used here to describe a mixed economy which has a large capitalist element. 'Private enterprise' is most conveniently regarded as the slogan of those who wish any shift in the frontiers between the state and private sectors to be in favour of the private one. A 'free economy' is a much looser term which perhaps suggests a combination of several of the other elements – a competitive capitalist market economy making maximum use of the price mechanism.

The 'market economy' is the most fundamental of all the concepts. As a first approximation, it can be said to describe a state of affairs in which those who own the means of production, distribution and exchange, as well as workers and consumers, pursue their own freely chosen ends rather than some supposed national good. The 'price mechanism' refers to an important part

[61]

of the mechanism by which a market economy (and perhaps also some other types of economy) function and individual decisions are reconciled with one another.

A market economy can consist largely, or even entirely, of state-owned enterprises, provided that those who run them are allowed to respond to consumer demand and do not have to follow some politically determined 'plan'. Because managers of such state concerns do not have a personal stake in their success, they cannot be left entirely free to pursue their own ends, and our provisional definition has to be modified. Some very general instructions such as 'maximise profits' may have to be given; and they may be reinforced by linking managerial remuneration with results. Managers running private concerns on behalf of shareholders have also to identify themselves artificially with a quest for profits which largely go to others; and similar conflicts of interest may arise. The opposite of a market economy is a *command economy,* in which the decision about what to produce, and how much, depends not on market demand but orders from the centre. The terminology is, interestingly enough, derived from discussion of Communist bloc countries, where elements of a market economy have had to be reintroduced in uneasy combination with the command element.

Trade and the 'zero-sum' game

The basic insight behind the case for the market economy is that *under certain conditions* the self-interest of one human being *can* further the welfare of other human beings. In contrast to much popular belief, trade is not a 'zero-sum game' like chess. *Both* parties to a transaction can benefit. The *profit motive* is a special case of the use of self-interest as a guiding force. The action of workers in seeking the employment with the best available combination of pay, working conditions and leisure is another. As Adam Smith put it long ago, we rely on the self-interest of the baker to provide our daily bread. Moreover, the forces of competition will encourage him to develop new types of bread and cheaper methods of baking, and prevent him from exploiting the consumers by obtaining an above-normal rate of return.

The invisible hand

It is well known that the 'invisible hand' will work reasonably well only if certain conditions are fulfilled. There is a fair degree of consensus among economists both about what they are and about the kinds of corrective that may be appropriate if they are not fulfilled. The statement of the conditions for a social optimum does indeed fill a great many textbooks. The basic tautology from which the others are derived is, in Dr Mishan's words, that 'the social value of the marginal product of each distinguishable factor is the same in all its existing uses'.[1] In other words, the additional value produced by every worker or raw material or piece of machinery should be equal. This means that there will be nothing to gain from shifting any productive agent from its present to another occupation.

Much high-grade intellectual effort has been devoted both to refining *optimum* conditions, which are never likely to be fulfilled, and to establishing that nothing can be said in general terms about the principles of policy unless all the optimum conditions are fulfilled (a proposition which is itself a subject of dispute among economists). It would be Luddite to decry the logical and mathematical exercises which lead to such results. But to use them as a blunderbuss to undermine all policy prescriptions by economists is to leave the field open to any charlatan, demagogue, interest group spokesman, or vote-bidder whose standards of argument are infinitely below those of the average working economist at his shakiest.

In spite of all the difficulties that exist at the most rarefied level, there is a body of 'informal welfare economics' which economists use in discussing real-world problems. There is a great deal of evidence, including the survey cited (p. 51), which suggests that two competent economists of different political views are likely to be much nearer in their approach to many problems than either would be to an intelligent layman, innocent of economics, who shared his politics. Indeed, there is probably more agreement among economists on the circumstances in which the profit motive does and does not promote the public welfare than on apparently less political and more technical areas.

The success of a market economy will depend to a large extent on a monetary and fiscal framework which will minimise the likelihood of either slumps or runaway inflation. The best efforts of the financial authorities can, however, be undermined by union monopoly power, and this topic cannot be omitted from any economic policy agenda.

Externalities (neighbourhood effects)

The main discrepancies between the interest of individual citizens and the working of the profit motive, even in the absence of monopoly elements, arise from what are called, under alternative

[1] E. J. Mishan, *Welfare Economics: An Assessment*, North Holland Publishing Co., 1969, pp. 29, 85.

[63]

terminologies, 'external economies' or 'diseconomies' (sometimes referred to as 'externalities'), 'third party', 'spillover', or—most evocatively—'neighbourhood effects'. They arise as the unintended result of some other activity; their effects are indiscriminate and those responsible can neither charge for them if they are beneficial nor be forced to pay for the damage if they are harmful. Chemical products discharged into a river impose harm on a community downstream which does not enter into the profit and loss account of the firm concerned. An extra car coming into London imposes costs on all other cars and on the passenger transport system, for which the driver does not have to pay.

Many of these discrepancies can be corrected by general measures without either specific intervention or a 'central plan'. Competition can be encouraged by anti-trust laws or freer trading policies. Changes in the law could make firms liable for some of the 'disbenefits' they cause. Discrepancies between private costs and the 'spillover' costs imposed on others can be corrected by taxes and subsidies. For example, a motorist could be discouraged from coming into London by a congestion tax under which he would equate the marginal convenience of his journey with the marginal increase in congestion costs for everyone concerned and not just himself. This allows more freedom of choice between motorists of different tastes and needs than does prohibition or licensing. Almost by definition the most important of these neighbourhood effects occur in what is nowadays called 'the environment'.

Public goods

There is also a category of services known as 'public goods', which cannot be sold in the market because they cannot, for technical reasons, be provided in different quantities to different people in accordance with their preferences. One obvious example is defence; another is an urban park, which benefits both those who regard the fresh air and view as worth the cost and those who do not. In such goods a political decision has to be taken. 'Public goods' are like favourable spillovers which convey indiscriminate benefits. The main difference is that their effects are intended rather than accidental.

The range of pure public goods is narrower than is sometimes supposed. Many services which are treated as public goods, such as health, higher education and social security and parts of housing, are provided collectively, either for frankly paternalist reasons, or as a backdoor method of bringing about some desired redistribution of income. However non-paternalist he is, a market economist may still not be satisfied with the distribution of income thrown up by the market. His approach here would, however, be to put the emphasis on social benefits in cash, preferably through a negative income tax, rather than on 'free' services in kind.

Policy disagreements among economists of an anti-paternalist hue are at several levels. There are some quite important technical disagreements. A hoary old chestnut is whether one should subsidise industries with declining *long-run* unit cost curves (of which there are fewer than is commonly imagined). Another is whether the rate of interest thrown up by the market really does measure the community's true preference between present and future consumption, whether because of the lack of a fully developed forward market, or other reasons.[1] An interesting recent controversy concerns the value of what has been given the unfortunate label 'indicative planning'. This can be given a non-interventionist interpretation, as Professor James Meade has done, in the form of providing producers with informed guesses about the consequences of certain possible developments, *which they are then free to follow or not*.[2] The value of such projections and stipulated relationships is an empirical matter depending on the predictability of the relationships involved and the risks that the project may degenerate under political pressure into either an exercise in wishful thinking or attempted government by interest groups.[3]

The really important disagreements do not in all probability relate to these well-known technical issues, and still less to discrepancies between 'ideal' growth paths in some mathematical models and what happens in the real world. Just as it is a *non sequitur* to make out a case for non-intervention on the basis of some idealised version of a market economy, it is equally impermissible to base arguments for intervention on comparisons between messy, real-world markets and some ideal plan which could be introduced by an omniscient government free from interest

[1]The whole 'ecological' controversy about whether the growth of material production should be drastically curtailed to preserve a tolerable planet concerns vast 'neighbourhood effects' posited for some future date. Because these threats are remote in time and the growth of our knowledge of ways of meeting them cannot be predicted, the whole problem is shrouded in enormous uncertainty. The controversies are further compounded, however, by differences of view about how much weight to give to the welfare of generations yet unborn.

[2]J. E. Meade, *The Theory of Indicative Planning*, Manchester University Press, 1970.

[3]Some comments on British experience with indicative planning can be found in my *Steering the Economy*, 3rd Penguin edn., 1971, especially Chapters 4, 7 and 8.

groups and guided solely by disinterested concern for some non-paternalist conception of the public interest.[1]

Government intervention—the onus of proof

Major differences among economists often reflect different beliefs about where the onus of proof should be placed in deciding when to intervene in practical instances. As Professor Friedman remarks, some 'neighbourhood effects' can be conjured up to justify almost any conceivable act of intervention. Most economists would favour taxes and subsidies (and perhaps a few out-and-out prohibitions), when there are large and obvious spillover effects, and would support cost-benefit studies (hopefully of a more sensitive and civilised kind than some we have seen) when large projects with obvious environmental effects are being considered. But to go beyond this and advocate discretionary state intervention in every private sector activity involves all of at least the three following empirical judgements : (a) that the unpriced spillover effects are likely to be large in relation to the costs of intervention, (b) that officials will have enough knowledge of cost conditions and individual preferences, now and in the future, to improve on the unaided market outcome, and (c) and most important of all, that the Government action will not in practice be largely influenced by local, political and industrial pressures (or prestige considerations) which would lead to a worse result than that of the unaided market.[2]

Another kind of apparent disagreement is largely a matter of presentation. To the extent that there is a consensus on how the market works, it can be summarised for popular purposes in ways which are equally valid but which have a very different political flavour. One economist can say that the market economy works well given the right environmental policies; another, who holds identical views on practical policy issues, can emphasise how much intervention is required to correct the evils of uninhibited market forces. (We are still talking about any market economy and waiving the question whether it has to be capitalist or not.)

There is indeed an ambiguity about the way the term 'market economy' is used in current political and economic discussion. A libertarian writer may put forward a positive case for a market econ-

---

[1][Economists following Professor Harold Demsetz, then of the University of Chicago, speak of the 'Nirvana approach' to policy. ('Information and Inefficiency: Another Viewpoint,' *Journal of Law and Economics*, 1969.) —ED.]

[2][These and allied propositions are examined by Professor Steven Cheung of the University of Washington in a Hobart Paper for publication in late 1975. Like Professor Coase, Professor Cheung argues that externalities constitute, *per se*, no conclusive case for the replacement of the market by government.—ED.]

omy to emphasise the paternalist and anti-consumer bias of many interventionist policies, to show that 'production for profit' *need* not be the evil that is supposed in political demonology, and that the alternative slogan of 'production for use' is, on the most charitable interpretation, meaningless. Nevertheless, someone who talks about a market economy is widely understood to mean *laissez-faire*. To meet this difficulty, the German neo-liberals[1] have coined the term 'social market economy'. But, as Professor Hayek has pointed out, the word 'social' is not only vague and confusing, but also risks giving the impression that there are such things as higher purposes over and above the purposes of individuals.[2] It is probably best to avoid misunderstanding and to use the colourless expression, 'corrected market economy', to emphasise that appropriate policies are being followed to create a suitable environment in which the market can function, and that discrepancies between private and social costs and benefits are taken into account.

The price mechanism

The influence of prices on economic behaviour in most, if not all, known societies is an unavoidable technical fact of life, in no way dependent on the political philosophy of the person observing it. Most popular discussion about prices refers to the rate at which their average level (the cost of living) is rising; and economists struggling with the inflation conundrum are certainly conscious of this 'macro-economic' problem. They are also, however, at least as interested in another aspect of prices—that of prices of different goods and services relative to each other—the 'micro-economic' problem. Prices are here very broadly defined to include items such as wages, rents, interest rates and, indeed, the charge made for any commodity or service sold for money, or even barter.

Both the demand for and the supply of goods and services are normally assumed to be related to the incomes of those involved in the transactions and to the prices offered or asked, relative to the prices of other goods and services. The effect of price upon supply can be in either direction. An increase in wages for a large category of workers can lead either to more hours being put in (the 'price' or substitution effect), because work is now more attractive relative to leisure, or to less hours being put in, because a smaller number now suffice to provide a given target income (the 'income' effect). The more narrowly the category of work is defined

[1]And lately some British Conservatives, such as Sir Keith Joseph.
[2]Hayek, *Studies in Philosophy, Politics and Economics,* Routledge & Kegan Paul, 1967, Chapter 7.

the more likely is a higher price to lead to more effort. A general increase in agricultural workers' wages, relative to other occupations, could lead to fewer hours being put in per worker. It is also likely to lead to more people wishing to become agricultural labourers (or fewer people leaving the land than otherwise); and this may or may not outweigh the effects on hours per worker—the time-scale considered being of relevance here. What one can say with confidence is that an increase in the price expected to be realised for a particular foodstuff, relative to other foodstuffs and to the general price level, will lead to an increase in its output, even if it means switching agricultural labourers from other activities.

The demand for a product or service is normally expected to be smaller the higher the price, relative to the general price level. This relationship of the demand for a commodity to the price charged is a tautology if a person's (or a country's) money income is constant and a particular price varies. After all, if the price rises high enough, expenditure on an unchanged quantity of the commodity in question will absorb the whole of one's income. Although this tautology is interesting in some situations (for example, in the analysis of a devaluation), much more interesting is the sensitivity of the demand for a particular commodity to a change in its price when there is no change in real income (either because other prices move in a compensatory direction or because there are compensatory increases in money income). This pure 'price' or 'substitution' effect of differences in relative prices is an empirical phenomenon, which can be observed by watching a housewife in a supermarket. The degree of responsiveness to such relative price changes is a matter for observation rather than arm-chair reflection.

These are the briefest of sketches of relationships which are elaborated at considerable length in books on economic principles. The *price mechanism* refers not only to these properties of prices, but also to the way in which they can be used to bring some form of order and co-ordination into a wide range of human activities. The expression can refer both to the *spontaneous* adjustments of the market and to the deliberate *manipulation* of prices by political authorities to change the working of the market—whether in aid of individualist or more paternalist goals.

If we are talking of the major products of an advanced industrial society, and not of a few specialist markets or bazaars, it is mainly in the allocation of resources *in the long run* that the price mechanism has a major role. If there is a reasonable degree of competition and entry is free to newcomers, prices will bear a roughly similar ratio to costs, including the going rate of return on capital in different branches of the economy. Assuming a public policy which charges enterprises for the major 'neighbourhood' or 'spillover' costs absent from their accounts (and if possible rewards them for spillover benefits) and reasonably high employment, the resulting price structure will indicate to people the true alternatives that are open to society—how many refrigerators would have to be foregone to produce an additional motor car, the sacrifice in output of consumer goods that would make possible a given addition to the number of coach tours or National Park wardens, or the sacrifice of goods and services of all kinds required to make possible a given addition to leisure, and so on. In other words, the structure of relative prices gives some idea of what economists call the 'opportunity cost' of different goods and services.

Over the time horizon in question there is unlikely to be shortage or surplus; for we have been considering a period long enough for production to be increased to remedy any shortages and reduced to eliminate surpluses. Thus, the relative price structure not only indicates the *costs* of different items in terms of foregone alternatives, but also represents the *valuation* that consumers place on their marginal purchases. In this way the market system will produce, in suitable circumstances, the goods that people happen to want, rather than what some authority—or their fellow men —think they ought to have, in the light of prices that convey information about the true costs of the various alternatives.

For the system to work in this way there must be, in the long run, freedom to compete on all aspects of the service offered. The business apologist cannot be allowed to get away with saying that, despite the existence of a price ring, there is competition in 'quality' or fierce sales rivalry. The consumer is being deprived of the option of paying a lower price with less service by the collusive action of producers. Competition does not presuppose private ownership, although to introduce it into the state sector may require deliberate policies which will go against the grain of those most actively concerned and may run up against the statutory monopoly status enjoyed by industry-wide nationalised undertakings.

Perfect competition

This is a convenient place to dispose of the widespread fallacy that the case for the market economy depends on the existence of something called 'perfect competition'. This whole approach is based on an edifice of misunderstandings. 'Perfect' and 'imperfect', when applied to competition, are technical terms, not terms of praise or blame. 'Perfect competition' is said to exist when a firm faces a 'perfectly elastic' demand for its product. This means that it is responsible for such a small part of total supply, and the product is so standardised and the element of goodwill so small, that the firm can sell all it likes at the going market price. If it raises its prices even slightly it will lose all its customers; if it lowers them it would be overwhelmed with far more orders than it could supply.

This state of affairs prevails mainly in some produce and financial markets. But the concept of perfect competition was arrived at, not from an observation of such markets, but from an attempt to set out in mathematical form the theory of a competitive economy. Later economists then observed that under certain very restrictive conditions it would produce an 'optimum' pattern of output, with production of goods corresponding to consumer preferences, and each firm producing on a scale that gives it the lowest possible long-run production costs. The main conditions required for this to occur include static technology and static consumer preferences, and the exhaustion of all economies of scale at a small size of firm. They also include the absence of both direct and indirect taxes, which distort the choice between income and leisure.[1]

The degree of competition in a dynamic economy cannot be measured by reference to the yardstick of perfect competition. As Schumpeter long ago observed, the industries where progress has been most rapid are often dominated by large-scale firms far removed from perfect competition. The most effective kind of competition is from the 'new commodity, the new technology, the new source of supply, the new type of organisation'.[2] The threat of competition of this kind is a powerful influence on existing firms, particularly in oligopolistic situations such as the fibre or car industries. At any one time the existing firms are in a privileged position; but prolonged failure to improve products or introduce low-cost methods, or any attempt at monopoly pricing, would attract newcomers which would threaten their hold. This does not mean that the government should just stand aside. But the features to watch are the freedom of entry of newcomers into the industry, and imports into the country, as well as the laws relating to restrictive practices. Perfect competition is virtually useless as a yardstick here.

It is, of course, wrong to suppose that even in the most favourable cases, the self-adjusting price mechanism provides any sort of

[1]For a good account of these complications, I. M. D. Little, *A Critique of Welfare Economics,* Oxford University Press, 2nd edn., 1956.

[2]Joseph Schumpeter, *Capitalism, Socialism and Democracy,* Unwin University Books, first published in Britain in 1943, 12th impression 1970, p. 84.

optimum distribution of resources. The most that can reasonably be claimed is that with the aid of the corrective devices repeatedly emphasised in these pages, the price system provides a *rough and ready way* of making those who take economic decisions pay attention to people's preferences whether as consumers or workers, savers or investors, gamblers or insurers.

Nor does the departure of the pattern of prices from what would be the optimum in a static world, where we were satisfied with the distribution of incomes, matter all that much from the point of view of either prosperity or freedom. The key influence on either our prosperity or its rate of growth is not whether the price of a specified coach tour relative to a refrigerator is 11 :8 when it ought to be 8 :11. (Comparisons of exact cost-price relations are mainly of importance when comparing close substitutes, for example, alternative fuels.) What is important, both for freedom and for want-satisfaction, is that, if an increase in the demand for coach tours makes the activity more profitable, the supply of such tours should be allowed to respond and not be held back because some economic planners regard the manufacturing output as more important. The effectiveness of such responses, and the speed with which businessmen adopt the procedures that would pay them best and are already in use in the most advanced firms, has more bearing on the rate of growth than exactly how far from the ideal the existing pattern of prices, costs and profits happens to be. This kind of responsiveness to a given economic environment has been christened 'x-efficiency'—which is another way of saying that economists can tell us little about it.

Short-period and long-period adjustments

In the foregoing summary explanation I have been very careful not to suggest that prices are used to eliminate shortages or surpluses in any but a long-period sense. Day-to-day rationing by price is nowadays more the exception than the rule. Economic activity can be largely guided by market demand, yet prices may be fairly inflexible for many months at a time. Car firms may allocate popular models by 'waiting lists' rather than by raising prices, and they may reduce production of an unpopular car without experimenting with relative price changes. Branded products may be slow to change in price in response to market conditions. Firms with surplus labour are more likely to cease recruitment or declare redundancies than reduce wages, while those with labour shortages may hope to pick up unemployed labour without bidding against other firms. Thus, in the short run, shortages and surpluses may take the place of price changes as signalling devices.

Free markets and the price mechanism

Free markets can be said to exist where the price of an article is free to vary from day to day, or at least at very frequent intervals, in such a way as to equate supply and demand and clear the market. Examples include the stock market, the second-hand car market, many of the food and raw material exchanges, and the purchase and sale of houses. The 'perfect' markets are a special case of free markets where the product is standardised and no individual seller or buyer is big enough to exert a perceptible influence on the price. At the other extreme is the house market, or the art market, where the items on sale are differentiated and individual buyers and sellers have an all too perceptible influence on the going rate for an individual item.

The case for *free markets* depends on empirical judgements. Those who dislike free markets would claim that the short-term responsiveness of demand and/or supply to price changes is small; and that free prices generate large and disturbing fluctuations which are aggravated rather than smothered by speculative activity.

A perennial example of this controversy is that over exchange rates. The case for using the exchange rate mechanism to balance international payments in preference to controls or otherwise unnecessary deflation is a matter of principle. But the case for freely floating exchange rates, in place of adjustments of official parities, is a matter in the last resort to be judged empirically. Nearly all the serious studies that have been made suggest that the allegations that genuinely floating rates fluctuate widely and are disturbing to trade are central bankers' or businessmen's myths. Most of the alleged instances have either been of fixed rates under pressure, or of disturbances due to interference by the authorities with the functioning of the market, combined with the belief that rates would be fixed again after political haggles of uncertain outcome. Where genuinely free rates have moved rapidly, it has been due mainly to highly inflationary domestic policies, differing in intensity from country to country, which would in any case have brought about devaluations and revaluations.[1]

The trap to avoid in discussing all such questions is to compare the degree of instability of real-world free markets with some imagined, ideal smooth path of adjustment. A debating point sometimes made against floating rates is that share prices do not move smoothly, but exhibit pronounced fluctuations around their trend. There are reasons for expecting freely floating exchange

[1]This argument is developed in my *The Price of Economic Freedom,* Macmillan, 1970, which also contains a bibliography citing some of the empirical studies.

rates to fluctuate less than share or commodity prices;[1] but it is worth asking why those who make this point do not advocate either extensive official intervention to smooth out share fluctuations or the fixing of share prices by financial institutions, to be changed only where there is clear-cut evidence of a 'fundamental' imbalance of supply and demand (as happens on some overseas exchanges with lesser securities). Can it be that they are not so confident, after all, that the step-like movements resulting from such arrangements would lead to more stability (however that is defined) than real-world stock exchanges with all their faults?

Safety valves

A little reflection suggests however that, even outside the purely financial sector, the absence of free markets is only tolerable, from the point of view of either freedom or efficiency, because of the presence of safety valves. Someone on a waiting list for one car model can switch over to a close substitute, often imported; or he can use the second-hand market. Many consumer goods' producers aim to have a modest margin of unused capacity in a normal year so that production can be stepped up fairly quickly. The use of bonuses, overtime offers and all the other apparatus of 'wage drift' to entice new workers is well enough known; if some well-meaning 'incomes policy' or TUC-CBI agreement were to stop such payments, we should really know the meaning of economic crisis. The relatively free market which used to exist in furnished accommodation was of course pushed to very high levels by rent controls elsewhere; but without this safety valve many people would have been unable to find rented accommodation at all. Although the text-books may exaggerate the extent to which prices are set on a continuous market-clearing basis in a modern economy, the existence of a number of markets which do work in this way illustrates the possible advantages for consumer choice if they were encouraged rather than suppressed.

Government use of the price mechanism

So far the price mechanism has been described as a system of automatic adjustment. But it can also be used as a weapon of government policy. It can be used, for instance, to improve the market economy as an instrument for satisfying individual desires. Taxes or subsidies can be imposed where there are spillover costs or benefits which the unaided market does not take into account. Sometimes it may be possible to 'internalise' costs which are at

[1]Cited in *ibid.*, pp. 51–2.

present external—for example, by imposing an obligation to pay compensation at market values for various kinds of damage to other people's property or amenity. Even where it is impracticable to change the law in this way, a good cost–benefit study[1] will seek to assess the value that people affected place on the environmental losses from a proposed new project—either how much they would pay to stop it or how much they would need in compensation to waive their objections. The two approaches can yield very different results, but either is better than ignoring the environmental damage, or abstract debating on 'environment' versus 'growth' which ignores the technical trade-offs and the preferences of those concerned. The effect of a project on property values can also give a clue and, in default of other methods, survey data, properly interpreted, can help.[2]

Indeed, state intervention of all kinds, whether motivated by concern for the individual or more paternalist considerations, can employ the price mechanism. Special depreciation allowances or investment grants are in effect subsidies to investment—which may be justified as an offset to the deterrent against investment provided by the rest of the tax system. The Selective Employment Tax was a price mechanism technique for discouraging the shift from manufacturing to services. The Regional Employment Premium was designed as a subsidy to reduce the cost of labour to employers in the high unemployment areas.

Clear examples of the use of the price mechanism out of a paternalist desire to encourage some activities or discourage others include heavy taxes on drink and tobacco and subsidies for sports grounds. (One motive for such taxes may be revenue-raising, but the revenue-raisers could not get away with such heavy discrimination against particular goods if they could not cloak it as paternalist disapproval of 'social vices'.) The interesting point is that the price mechanism is a relatively *liberal means* of carrying out even *illiberal policies*, by comparison with prohibition and orders. State action will impart a bias against smoking and drinking and in favour of sport, compared with the unimpeded action of market forces; but individual behaviour will still vary according to personal tastes.

Pricing and standards

An interesting example of the use of the price mechanism as a relatively liberal means of control is the proposal by Professors

[1][The various forms of cost-benefit analysis are examined by Professor G. H. Peters in *Cost-Benefit Analysis and Public Expenditure*, Eaton Paper 8, IEA, 3rd edn., 1973.—ED.]

[2]On all this, E. J. Mishan, *Cost Benefit Analysis*, Allen & Unwin, 1971.

William Baumol and Wallace Oates for 'environmental standards', for example, to achieve a given level of purification of a river or to halve the level of sulphur dioxide emission into the atmosphere.[1] The justification for imposing these 'arbitrary' standards might be that here is an area where a measure of paternalism is justified— people affected by the widespread application of DDT might lack the technical knowledge to assess its harmful effects and put too low a monetary value on it; or it might be the simple, pragmatic one advanced by Professor Baumol that we do not know the marginal net valuation that people affected would put on the environmental spillover from various industrial activities, and the best we can do is to make a political guess about what the outcome would be if these adverse spillovers could be properly priced.

The interesting aspect of this proposal, which distinguishes it from similar proposals emanating from physical scientists, is that the required environmental standards would be obtained, not by regulations or prohibitions, but by levying a sufficient tax on all effluents poured into a river, which varied according to the organic waste-load of the effluent, or a tax on smoke emissions.

Professor Baumol justifies his use of the price mechanism approach on the ground that it is the least costly method of achieving the required standards. Those firms that can reduce smoke or effluent emission at relatively little cost will bear the bulk of the reductions; those for whom such reductions are very expensive or physically impossible will pay the tax (which may, via its effect on prices, reduce their total output).

But the argument could also be put in terms of freedom of choice. Taxes are set at a level which is found sufficient to achieve certain environmental standards; but the individual firm is given the choice how far it should pay the tax and how far it should reduce the quantity of its emissions. People who cannot bring themselves to attach any value at all to freedom for a firm (even though this is likely to benefit the employees as well as directors) have only to transfer the example to activities performed by individuals—taking cars into city centres, 'over-fishing' in rivers, the use of detergents which create disposal problems, and so on.

Economists and the price mechanism

A disposition to use the price mechanism is probably the most important single feature linking the policy views of economists of

[1]These proposals can be found in P. Bohm and A. Kneese (eds.), *The Economics of Environment*, Macmillan, 1971. As a spillover benefit the reader will find in the following chapter of that book an interview with Dr Pangloss on the pollution problem!

otherwise very varying persuasions. Many economists who are most sceptical of the workings of unimpeded free markets are strong proponents of correctives which work by influencing prices. Devaluation, the 'crawling peg', the Selective Employment Tax, the Regional Employment Premium, and parking meters are all price mechanism devices—in a way in which price *controls,* prohibitions, restrictions and quotas are not. This liberal bias of economists does not reflect any moral virtue, but the fact that their professional competence lies almost entirely in assessing functional relations between supply and demand and prices, income and wealth.

The price mechanism and the public

Unfortunately, the allocative functions of the price mechanism have never been understood by the general public, or even the politically conscious section of it. This is due partly to a confusion between the macro-economic goal of price stability (or minimum inflation), which relates to the general level of *all* prices, and micro-economic price *relativities* between goods (or occupations). Understanding has not been helped by the incessant exhortation involved in prices and incomes policies; a genuine difficulty is that the long-overdue correction of price relativities—which in practice often means an increase in the prices of basic services such as fuel or rent—will, when other prices are sticky, not merely lead to a once-for-all rise in the general price level, but may under a permissive monetary policy also trigger off a continuous process of cost inflation.

Nevertheless, it is doubtful if the confusion caused by the inflationary issue entirely explains the public hostility to the use of the price mechanism and its attachment to the medieval idea of a 'just price'. One obvious objection is distributional : that a change in relative prices always makes some people worse off relative to others. This is rationalised by saying that the poor usually suffer if price, instead of administrative allocation or queuing, is used as a rationing device—rents or school meals being stock examples.

There are, of course, other ways of offsetting any adverse distributional effect of relative price changes by means of the tax and social security system.[1] Moreover, it is doubtful if the price mechanism would gain much in people's affections even if it were clear that its use would not shift the distribution of income against the poor. One did not notice much enthusiasm for the use of metering devices to price scarce road space in towns. (One of the

[1] Discussed in VI, pp. 111–113.

first such meters entered a room in Ernest Marples' house via a broken window!) It is tempting to be patronising and talk about the low level of economic literacy among voters, but I am afraid that hostility to the price mechanism and belief in the just price reflect a deeper illiberalism.[1]

III. THE CORRECTED MARKET ECONOMY

Freedom or prosperity?

The goal of the 'corrected' market economy can very loosely be regarded as aiming to secure a combination of freedom of choice and prosperity. The two are certainly not the same but are not all that easy to disentangle because, once we cease to be mesmerised by the veil of money, prosperity is an even more difficult concept to unravel than freedom; and the problem is not solved by using more technical-sounding terms such as 'aggregate real income' or 'economic welfare'. It is worth asking to what extent different types of infringements of the ideals of the corrected market economy are infringements of freedom and to what extent they are simply holding down the level of prosperity.

Let us start with an example heavily weighted towards the anti-prosperity side, the subsidisation of one fuel so that its ratio of price to marginal cost differs very markedly from that of close substitutes and where there are no discrepancies between private and social costs of a type that justify such different pricing policies. Now, there is an element of interference with free choice in this operation. If one believes that coercion is a matter of degree, the consumer is being pushed by government into buying more of one fuel and less of another than he would like. But even if there are numerous examples of these distortions in the economy, the effects on freedom are relatively trivial; and the issues are to be regarded as ones of industrial policy rather than human liberty. In assessing the degree of freedom that exists in the society, we should give them little weight compared with questions such as whether conscription exists, the degree of coercion practised on minors, the extent of civil liberties and the absence or presence of censorship.

But we should pause a moment before dismissing such instances altogether even if our main concern is with freedom rather than industrial efficiency. Freedom of choice of occupation and freedom to spend one's money in one's own way are vital freedoms of the negative kind. A system in which a 'Control of Engagements Order' was enforced (as Diocletian attempted more successfully

[1]Discussed further, VI, *passim*.

than the Labour Government of 1947) or where a great many activities, which did not harm other people, were prohibited or restricted by severe rationing, would take us far on the road to serfdom. As Professor Fritz Machlup points out, a dictator who wished to decide what it was good for people to consume and which occupations they should follow, could, in theory, achieve his aims by an extreme manipulation of the price mechanism. He could set very high prices for products of which he disapproved and very low ones for those he liked; he could ordain very low wages for some 'undesirable' activities and high ones for 'virtuous' activities.[1] The resulting heavy losses in some occupations could be offset by subsidies. This would be a less unfree society than one in which individual people were told which jobs to do, an example of our earlier dictum that the price mechanism can be a liberal means even of carrying out illiberal policies. Nevertheless, the society could hardly be regarded as other than a highly regimented one.

Value of fringe markets

At what stage 'perverse' intervention in the market economy becomes a serious threat to freedom is a matter of fine judgement— and of interest even to those who could not care less about the GNP or economic growth. I would attach a good deal of value to the fringe free markets, such as that in furnished accommodation or in the phenomenon of wage drift, where market clearing prices are allowed to operate. Their suppression, which a misguided reforming government might attempt at any time, would be a serious narrowing of the range of choice otherwise open to people, compared with which the muddles over energy prices or the road-rail fare structure are of minor importance.

A clear example of misguided interference with the market economy, which is of more importance for freedom of choice than for prosperity, is foreign travel restrictions. An instance of blindness to the economic aspects of freedom was the readiness of a government to impose as recently as 1966 a travel allowance which virtually confined Britons to this country, except for a cheese-paring vacation, as a cheap political gesture. Yet one of the severest restrictions it is possible for governments to impose on personal liberty in time of peace, which remained in operation for over three years, was greeted with hardly a word of protest from many professed libertarians, a large number of whom had ample opportunity of travel for official, business or cultural purposes.

[1] F. Machlup, 'Liberalism and the Choice of Freedoms', in E. Streissler (ed.), *Roads to Freedom,* Routledge & Kegan Paul, 1969.

Such restrictions on foreign travel have an adverse effect on prosperity, real incomes and living standards; but this is very much a secondary aspect. It is perfectly possible to imagine a situation where there is a political veto on devaluation, or where the adverse effects on the terms of trade of a successful devaluation are believed to be very severe, and in which the imposition of a stringent travel allowance makes possible an expansion in output, income and employment, which for most people more than compensates for the travel curbs; and the total package may not have an adverse impact on the relative position of the poor, but even improve it. Yet a severe diminution of personal liberty remains—just as it would if bribes were paid to people to vote for the censorship of political views, resulting in a majority in favour of the measures—a majority who would, by definition, be 'better off' as, given the choice, they had preferred the bribes to free speech.

Both the strength and the limitations of the 'corrected' market economy can be illustrated by the perennially topical example of 'lame duck' industries. The Conservative Government after the 1970 General Election set out the case for not propping up such industries in the most unconvincing and repellent form possible. Whether intentionally or not, Ministers gave the impression that imposing discomforts on those managing or working in unprofitable industries was almost desirable in itself because it would 'wake people up to their responsibilities'. They seemed to take positive pleasure in the prospect that life would be 'less cosy' or 'less comfortable' in activities for which state support was to have been withdrawn.

These unpleasant effects are drawbacks, not advantages. The real argument against supporting loss-making activities, which cannot justify themselves on the basis of demonstrable spillover benefits, is the harm that such support inflicts on the material welfare and on the freedom of choice of consumers. Protective devices for lame-duck industries force the rest of the population to purchase goods from a particular source, and to make sacrifices in their living standards for the sake of privileged producer groups. Moreover, if there is any mobility of labour or facilities for re-training and opportunities for jobs elsewhere, the gains to the protected group will diminish over time. Given that we are all consumers and anyone may find himself a lame duck, it is probable that a mutual understanding to abjure these make-work policies (as in Social Democratic Sweden), together with generous financial assistance for those making the readjustment, would be in the best interests of most people including the lame ducks themselves.

Although the above argument puts the emphasis on the loss of potential material welfare, the freedom aspect is not negligible. All taxation is a form of coercion—albeit of a negative kind—in that it prevents an individual spending a portion of his income in his own way. If taxation approached 100 per cent and people had to depend on supplies provided collectively, the degree of coercion would be very high indeed. But a lesser degree of taxation is a necessary evil if we are to enjoy the benefits of 'public goods'. The relationship between taxation and coercion is not one for one. A large amount of freedom can exist in a society where the average person pays 20 per cent of his income in tax. A significant erosion has taken place if this proportion rises to 40 per cent, but we could still be talking about a largely free society. At 60 per cent rates it would not be hysterical to say that people's choices were being largely made for them by the state; and at an 80 per cent rate the society would be a free one only in name.[1] Subsidies out of taxation for aerospace products, high technology computers or shipyards for which there is no commercial demand are, other things being equal, a restriction on people's freedom to spend their money in their own way; and if it is superimposed on a state of affairs where tax rates tend to be in the 30–40 per cent bracket in any case, it has to be very carefully justified by some countervailing material benefit either to some deserving group or to the population as a whole.

Compensating the victims of change

Reference to 'generous financial assistance' to the victims of change does expose an inherent difficulty as soon as we come to ask 'How generous?' The aim should be to provide as much as possible of what people say that they want in the light of correct information about 'opportunity costs'. But in real-world changes some people will lose and others gain. To overcome this difficulty, the concept of a 'potential Pareto improvement' has been invented for a change in which the gains *could* be so redistributed that no-one is worse off and some people are better off.

Unfortunately the concept of a potential improvement is very ambiguous. Apart from the numerous scholastic paradoxes that fill the literature, the state of the law can make a very real difference to whether a change appears as a potential Pareto improvement or not. A good example is the construction of a new airport. It is quite possible that the maximum sum that the in-

[1]The percentage should, strictly speaking, be net of cash benefits returned to citizens to spend as they like. For some discussion of actual magnitudes, see my chapter in B. Crick and W. A. Robson (eds.), *Taxation Policy*, Penguin Books, 1973.

dividuals of the area—if they could be properly mobilised—would be prepared to pay to the airport authority not to go ahead would be insufficient to stop construction on a profit-and-loss calculation. So it would look as if the gains exceeded the losses and that the airport represented a potential Pareto improvement. The inhabitants could still be compensated by paying them what they would have been prepared to pay to stop the airport.

Now let us suppose that the airport authority is not entitled to go ahead without the consent of the inhabitants. A very much larger sum might be required; so large that the airport would not be built. It would then look as if the losses exceeded the gains and the airport did not represent a Pareto improvement at all. It is not fanciful to suppose that, even if all the inhabitants could be properly organised and could suppress their sense of outrage at the request, they would be able and willing to pay only, say, £20 million, to stop an airport being built, while if they themselves had the right of veto even £100 million would not be enough to persuade them.[1]

Clearly, the wider the range of legal liability and the larger the number of changes which are allowed to take place only on payment of compensation that the victims consider adequate, the slower will be the pace of material change. The wealthier a society becomes the stronger the case for shifting the onus of compensatory payments onto those who want to make the change. For the harm caused by disturbing people's expectations and patterns of life must loom larger, the higher the whole community is above the poverty line and the less urgent the total growth of output.

There are, nevertheless, difficulties in going the whole hog with Dr Mishan and giving full legal rights to the victims of change. There is the obvious incentive to lie or exaggerate. If I have a veto over the construction of an airport, I would be tempted to ask for far more than the sum of money genuinely required to compensate me for the loss I would suffer. But, even if absolute sincerity could be guaranteed, what would be the situation of an old lady who does not believe in the hereafter, who finds that her life would be shattered either if the airport were built or if she had to move? (Sound insulation would be no use, as she has to sit out in the fresh air.) She might rationally regard the whole of the national income of the UK as insufficient compensation.

Transfer this example to a shipyard threatened with closure. Imagine a worker unwilling or too old to retrain, but whose pride would be hurt by being out of work and who would prefer to

[1]For elaboration of these points, Mishan, *Cost Benefit Analysis, op. cit.*, especially Chapters 18 and 29.

continue in his present job at his present wage, even if offered an immensely large capital sum as an alternative. The principle of compensation to victims of change has to be watered down in some common-sense way to what the majority of those concerned could be reasonably expected to accept. It was often said half-jocularly by the officials and executives involved that it might be cheaper to pay each man now employed £1,000 per annum until retirement, or a lump sum of £10,000, than to keep a particular mine, shipyard or aircraft project going. If this is really so, it would surely be better to pay compensation and close down the operation.

With large and obvious changes, such as the closing down of a shipyard or an aircraft firm, there will be strong support for actual rather than potential compensation to the victims of change. It is unfortunate that the likelihood of this happening will depend on the publicity generated and emotional appeal of the issue for the media; and one would prefer to see more systematic machinery which could help many victims of smaller changes that do not achieve the same publicity, but which often cause far more human hardship. Nevertheless, complete compensation of all victims of change would be of doubtful desirability. An anti-interventionist would always be able to argue that the choice of occupation is itself a gamble, and full compensation would involve subsidising high-risk activities. His opponent could reply that the ordinary worker cannot choose but take the gamble that is associated with a choice of job, and therefore be confronted with a non-insurable risk. Complete compensation, even as an ideal solution, should apply only to those below a certain income or wealth level, and should not apply to shareholders who are knowingly engaged in providing 'risk capital'.

But, even qualified in this way, full compensation to all victims of change is never likely to be practicable. Differences in attitudes among economists often depend on how far the economist insists that there should be an *actual*, as distinct from a *potential*, 'Pareto improvement'. One reason for the hostility to market forces of some unquestionably anti-paternalist economists arises from a preoccupation with income distribution so extreme that changes caused by market forces will not be accepted without cast-iron guarantees that the less well-off will be invariably and fully compensated for any adverse impact they might conceivably suffer. A more middle-of-the-road, and also more reasonable, position is to support market remedies, except where the adverse distributional implications are large and unambiguous and it is clear that compensation will not be paid. In other cases it would be best to favour measures likely to provide prosperity and freedom of choice, while keeping a watch on the general distribution of income and urging appropriate fiscal changes if this seems to be moving in an undesired direction. One wonders what the position of the less well-off would be if the cast-iron guarantee approach had been used to block all the changes of the last 150 years.

Intervention in labour markets

The biggest menace to a free society is not so much any brand of egalitarianism but the contention that relative rewards should depend on a political assessment of how much an occupation is worth. The objection is not, of course, to selection or promotion 'on merit', particularly in large organisations, where the implied contrast is with nepotism. The objection is to the contention that rewards of different individuals should depend on some sort of *collective* judgement of 'society' of what they are worth.

As Professor Hayek points out,

'no man or group of men possesses the capacity to determine conclusively the potentialities [the deserts and opportunities] of other human beings and . . . we should certainly never trust anyone invariably to exercise such a capacity.'[1]

To assess merit presupposes that a man has acted in accordance with some accepted rule of conduct and that someone else can judge how much effort and pain this has cost him. Often, of course, a highly meritorious attempt may be a complete failure, while a valuable human achievement will be due to luck or favourable circumstances. To decide on merit

'presupposes that we can judge whether people have made such use of their opportunities as they ought to have made, and how much effort of will or self-denial it has cost them and how much of their achievement is due to circumstances'.[2]

This is impossible in a free society or probably at all. Moreover, only a fanatical ascetic would wish to encourage a maximum of merit in this sense. It is more rational for people 'to achieve a maximum of usefulness at a minimum of pain and sacrifice and therefore a minimum of merit'.

Hayek is also right to insist that in a free society a man's livelihood does not depend on other people's valuation of his merit. It is sufficient that he should be able to perform some work or sell

[1]Hayek, *The Constitution of Liberty*, Routledge & Kegan Paul, 1960, pp. 88 *et seq.*

[2]Hayek, *ibid.*

a service for which there is a demand. He concedes that as an organisation grows larger it will become inevitable that ascertainable merit in the eyes of managers (or some conventional seniority structure) should determine rewards. But so long as there is no one single organisation with a comprehensive scale of merit, but a multiplicity of competing organisations with different practices (as well as smaller organisations and a self-employed sector), an individual still has a wide degree of freedom of choice.

There is, indeed, a still stronger argument against reward by merit which should influence even 'pragmatists' who do not attach any special value to personal choice. This is that there simply does not exist in modern Western states a sufficiently wide consensus on the relative merits or deserts of occupations and groups. However resentful they are about it, people will in the last resort accept a relatively low position in the pecking order if it is due to the luck of the *impersonal market,* or even the greater success of other groups in their monopolistic activities. They may retaliate by organising monopolistic associations of their own to engage in industrial stoppages; but they will recognise that no ultimate judgement has been pronounced. If, on the other hand, their low position seems to result from a moralistic evaluation of their merits made by their fellow citizens through some *political* process—whether by individual *persons* in the Government or on boards appointed for the task—they will stop at nothing to get the judgement withdrawn. No one likes being consigned to the rubbish heap by a body of identifiable wise men appointed to express the supposed moral evaluations of society. Some evidence for this contention is provided by the much greater political bitterness surrounding public sector than private sector wage disputes, as recent examples running all the way from coal-miners to doctors and London teachers testify.

Incompatibility of reward by merit and equality

An interesting feature of the argument against reward by merit is that it ought to be entirely acceptable to a strict egalitarian. The incompatibility of the two ideas of equality and reward according to merits comes out very clearly in one of the few coherent statements of the egalitarian case to have appeared in recent years, Mr Douglas Jay's *Socialism and the New Society.*[1] There the author clearly states that no man or woman has a greater 'right to happiness' than any other and the fact that people are born 'with an endless variety of character, intelligence, energy and ability, is morally irrelevant to this assertion'.

[1]Longmans, 1962.

An egalitarian could easily find a full-blown system of merit assessment even more distasteful than the present mixture of market and traditional status-determined differentials.

'A society in which it was generally presumed that a high income was proof of merit and a low income lack of it, in which it was universally believed that position and remuneration correspond to merit, in which there was no other road to success than the approval of one's conduct by the majority of one's fellows, would probably be much more unbearable to the unsuccessful ones than one in which it was frankly recognised that there was no necessary connection between merit and success.'

This is a quotation from Hayek's *The Constitution of Liberty*, but it could equally have come from an egalitarian socialist inveighing against the meritocracy and arguing against equality of opportunity as an inadequate ideal.

Payment by merit and direction of labour

Hayek argues that payment by 'merit' would mean that market valuations of a man's activities would provide him with no guidance about where to use his talents and what risks to undertake. He would have to be told what to do by someone else : in other words, explicit or implicit direction of labour. Here, however, we must be careful. Direction of labour is a plausible result if the principle is pushed too far. But how far is 'too far', and what exactly happens, will depend on policy decisions other than the decision to pay according to 'merit'. If, for example, it was decided that a nurse's 'merit' exceeded her market rate of pay, there would be a surplus of girls seeking to enter the profession, and some who had previously come up to standard would be rejected by a selection procedure, thus increasing the discretionary power of the hospital authorities over the careers of those concerned. The effects on the employment of nurses would, however, probably be less than in other occupations because most nurses are remunerated out of rates and taxes.

In the commercial sector, an increase in relative pay for, say, copper-plate workers, would not only increase the number of job applicants but would also reduce employment opportunities. If half the jobs in the country were upgraded on a 'merit' basis and the other half downgraded, there would be an exodus of employees from the high 'merit' occupations, where jobs would be chronically scarce, to the low 'merit' ones, where they would be plentiful but ill-rewarded. The only way of avoiding these paradoxical effects would be for the state to give large and expensive subsidies to the favoured trades and/or put heavy taxes on the least favoured ones, thereby substituting a politically determined pattern of output for that preferred by consumers.

But restrictive though all this is of freedom of consumer choice, it need not amount to direction of labour. The latter would be necessary only if the state begrudged paying the subsidies and raising the taxes, but was not prepared to accept a redistribution of workers towards the low 'merit' occupations. State action to protect from adverse market forces the pay of a *group* that stood high in public esteem—whether engine drivers facing the rundown of the rail system or teachers when there is a glut of graduates—would not take us along the road to serfdom. But an *across-the-board* system of merit evaluation (e.g. paying lavatory attendants more than university professors and dustmen more than stockbrokers) would lead to such an unacceptable allocation of resources (involving, for example, high unemployment among the lavatory attendants) and the necessary subsidies would be so unpopular (and themselves another source of distortion of the choice between work and leisure) that widespread compulsion would be an all too likely result.

The alternative to payment by merit is payment according to the market value of a person's activities—*as modified by whatever fiscal action is taken to alter the distribution of income and wealth*. We do not need to be starry-eyed about the character of this market value. It will be influenced by the attempts of professional associations and trade unions to restrict supply, as well as by traditional views of proper scales. If the suppy of clergymen suitable for promotion to archbishop exceeds the demand, the archepiscopal stipend will not, in the short run, be reduced (although it may be less quickly adjusted to compensate for inflation). In other words, it will be a highly imperfect market system in which rewards will not only depend on the mixture of luck, skill, opportunity and monopoly power characteristic of markets, but also on arbitrary traditional relativities, which themselves represent the lagged influences of the market relativities of a generation or two ago.

Disparities and inequalities imposed by artificial barriers to entry should be reduced where possible. We should be extremely sceptical of the monopolistic claims made by the medical or legal profession, as of the restrictive practices of the craft unions. These nowadays include the National Union of Journalists, which has imposed restrictive conditions—such as experience in the provinces—on entry into Fleet Street, over and above those which editors would have considered necessary if left to themselves. To the extent that there are professional skills involved, which the layman is not qualified to judge, it should be sufficient for the state to establish a register of qualified persons, leaving it to the consumer to decide whether to go by this register or to seek unqualified help.

Above all, we should be suspicious of the attempts of more and more occupations, whether advertising, management or journalism, to emulate the professions and to set up obstacle courses in the shape of examination requirements or 'on the job training', confining entry to graduates, or similar limitations. To the extent that these new qualifications and courses produce results, employers or members of the public using the services will give preference to those holding them. To restrict the activities in question to those so qualified, by law or collective agreement, is a pure exercise of coercion to establish a monopoly position. Yet at the end of the day, even if we are relatively unsuccessful in fighting off these evils, we should still regard a pattern of awards determined politically by governmental action, or demagogic use of the organs of publicity, as a cure far worse than the disease.

IV. MARKET ECONOMY—CAPITALIST OR SOCIALIST?

It is time to move on from considering the types of correction a market economy requires to the question, so far left aside, of whether a successful market economy needs to be based on *capitalism*. The converse is certainly untrue : capitalism need not involve a market economy. Not only can a system of private ownership of the means of production be highly uncompetitive, but it can even be a *command economy*. The decisions of individual capitalists can be subject to highly detailed instructions given at the discretion of the country's rulers (as in Nazi Germany) or by some central organisation of the capitalists themselves. Historically, however, capitalism has tended more often than not to be associated with a market economy and there are powerful forces impelling it in that direction.

The opposite of capitalism is, of course, socialism; it will be convenient to define it in the old-fashioned way as state ownership of the means of production, distribution and exchange. There was a lengthy debate among academic economists in the inter-war and wartime years on whether it was possible to have a socialist market economy. Echoes of that debate have continued in some of the writings on the economics of public enterprise. The conclusions seem to hang on whether a *dynamic* or *static* approach is used.

There is no reason why an economy consisting entirely of state-owned enterprises should not provide a *known* set of goods according to the signals provided by the market-place. Indeed, it could probably improve upon private enterprises by decreeing that managers must ignore any element of monopoly power and relate prices to marginal costs more closely than is likely in existing capitalist concerns. The problems of 'externalities' and spillover would, however, remain, and would have to be dealt with by some combination of price incentives and deterrents and administrative controls, as in capitalist economies.

Where, however, it is a matter of *discovering* what is the lowest cost method (rather than finding a position on a *known* cost curve) or of inventing products or services for meeting *changing* needs and tastes, the matter is wholly different. How is a limited amount of investment funds to be allocated among everybody with a bright idea? Or indeed, who are to be the managers and who the managed? It is no use applying a standard discounting technique to *future* costs and receipts and allocating funds to projects expecting the highest return. For both the receipts and the costs are precisely what are in dispute between the rival claimants.

If all investment funds went through one insurance company and were lent to firms consisting entirely of salaried managers with no personal stake in their concerns, the same problems would arise in a capitalist society. But, fortunately, this is not yet the case. Not only are the lending decisions made by different institutions, but the existence of personal private capital allows people to try out their own pet ideas, either with their own funds, or by using their assets as security for further loans. Even when it comes to reinvestment by existing firms, each management can try to prove the validity of its own ideas, however unorthodox, about the returns from alternative ventures, knowing that it is accountable to its own shareholders and can be thrown out by a takeover bid. Such individual hunches would be more difficult to justify to an enlarged National Enterprise Board, acting as trustee for *all* the nation's investment funds.

A socialist market economy is still better from the point of view of consumer satisfaction than a socialist command economy, even though it is probably less imaginative than a capitalist one in developing new techniques, products and services. This explains why the economic reforms designed to bring in the profit motive and relate prices more clearly to meaningful costs have led to improvements in Eastern Europe, but why a generally dowdy impression remains and why there is such a strong desire to borrow Western techniques.

Nationalised industry and competition

The nationalised industries in the West, and above all in the UK, have suffered from their symbolic role in 'left' – 'right' politics. This has led to a campaign of ridicule and denigration on the one side and partisan point-scoring on the other. At the time of writing left-wing politicians and academics are fond of pointing to a large book by R. W. S. Pryke,[1] which claims to have shown that, not only have the UK nationalised concerns performed better than private manufacturing industry, but that this is the direct result of nationalisation. This provoked a rebuttal by George and Priscilla Polanyi.[2] The argument was partly on the suitability of output per man-hour as an indicator of performance, and on whether Mr Pryke had made adequate allowance for the effects of the very much larger input of new capital per head into the state sector. Also at issue were the effects of the inclusion of the fast-growing electricity and airways industries in the state sector. These industries have shown rapid productivity gains relative to manufacturing industry in most countries, irrespective of ownership. It was, in the end, difficult to believe that anything had been 'proven' by either side.[3]

The one point that did emerge and that was common to both parties was that there had been a large *relative* improvement in the performance of the state sector between the decades 1948–58 and 1958–68. This was related to two phenomena : (a) the loss of effective monopoly power as other sources of energy and transport emerged to compete with state undertakings, and (b) the adoption of a much more commercial approach to the nationalised industries, in which they were given target rates of return, pressed to relate prices more closely to marginal costs and to use modern techniques of investment appraisal, and, above all, given specific subsidies for any loss-making services that they were expected to run.

Even if one accepts that the nationalised industries are capable of putting up a comparable performance to private business in established industries, this tells us nothing whatsoever about how

[1] *Public Enterprise in Practice,* MacGibbon & Kee, 1971.

[2] 'The Efficiency of Nationalised Industries', in *Moorgate and Wall Street Review,* Spring 1972.

[3] [The economic arguments for and against nationalisation and other forms of government control of industry are analysed in Ivy Papps, *Government and Enterprise,* Hobart Paper 61, IEA, 1975. – ED.]

capital would be allocated between *new* and untried industries and ventures (and individuals wanting to run them) in a completely state-run economy. It is no accident that, this side of the Iron Curtain, the industries that tend to be state-run are either old-established basic ones, such as the railways, buses or coal, or state-subsidised, prestige technology activities such as aerospace and atomic energy. On the other hand, where change is rapid, but not of a broadly predictable kind, and personal contact with consumers or dispersed local knowledge important—such as the retail trade, travel agencies or the profitable end of electronics—private ownership tends to prevail. In the rare cases where state concerns thrive in such trades, it is under the stimulus of strong competition from privately owned rivals.

In sectors which fall between the two extremes (notably posts and telecommunications), the performance of state monopolies seems, to put it mildly, undistinguished. Some of the most controversial aspects concern the quality of service given to the customer, which is not easily captured by productivity indices. The personal incentive to try out new ideas and respond flexibly to changing consumer demands is normally less in a state enterprise trying to ape capitalist practice than in the genuine article. Not only is there less to gain from success, but there is less to lose from failure. (Salaried managers in large bureaucratic companies suffer from similar drawbacks, but to a smaller degree.) As Patrick Hutber observed in relation to the Post Office Corporation's attempts in 1970–71 to imitate what it thought was correct commercial behaviour, 'You don't make a bear into a tiger by painting stripes upon its back'.[1]

The stock example, constantly quoted against such generalisations, is the more adventurous spirit shown by the IRI state-holding group in Italy. This has been achieved by removing many of the political constraints which, in a country like the UK, govern public enterprise.[2] The heads of the Italian organisation are given a degree of power without responsibility, which we should rightly hesitate to let such men have. The situation was made tolerable by the fact that state concerns had, up to the beginning of the 1970s, complete monopoly in very few fields and were usually subject to private competition, especially from imports. Should this situation change, as it shows signs of doing, the character of the Italian state sector would be likely to undergo a corresponding transformation. There have, in fact, been signs in

[1] 'Letter Box Lunacy', *Sunday Telegraph*, 7 November, 1971.
[2] [A study of the IRI and the lessons for Britain by an Italian economist is in Mario Deaglio, *Private Enterprise and Public Emulation*, Research Monograph 5, IEA, 1966. – ED.]

several countries of a new role for public ownership and participation—that of saving from liquidation private concerns such as Rolls-Royce[1] that have failed the test of the market, and which can offer no favourable spillovers to justify their subsidisation. This kind of safety net gave the worst of both capitalist and socialist worlds; yet it was welcomed by the less thinking socialists on the grounds that it extended the state sector and showed that 'private enterprise does not work'.

The improvements in the main British nationalised industries were threatened in the early 1970s by a Conservative Government which used them as political instruments in a way that the more crudely interventionist Labour Ministers would dearly love, but are sometimes prevented from doing by the Treasury. Examples included arm-twisting to make the nationalised industries conform to the CBI price restraint pledge of 1971, when they had not been allowed to rebuild their profit margins and were remote from fulfilling their financial objectives. This was followed by pressure to invest in unprofitable directions as part of the Government's reflationary drive. These and many other weaknesses have been pointed out by Christopher Foster in what is much the most perceptive study of the subject available.[2] Foster seems, however, to regard all these misfortunes as being due to remediable errors of particular governments, and puts forward excellent proposals for clarifying objectives and returning to the previous emphasis on profitability. Yet what shines out from his own account is that their nationalised status put these undertakings in the political arena irrespective of the White Papers written by Whitehall economists; and sooner or later any government is going to manipulate them—not to achieve some subtle adjustment between private and social costs or returns, but for short-run political objectives.

A market in intellectual property

So far this exposition has concentrated on the connection between the capitalist market economy and economic freedom and welfare. But many of its most forceful advocates have prized it at least as much as a precondition for intellectual freedom. The argument is well known. In a capitalist society means are available to advocate socialism (or pacificism or numerous other heresies). Ideas in the forms of books, newspaper articles, plays, films, as well as in more subtle and less obvious forms are sold on the open market; and *the more the profit motive operates* the less a publisher will be influenced by his personal attitudes to the views expressed.

[1] And now British Leyland.

[2] C. D. Foster, *Public Enterprise,* Fabian Research Series No. 300, 1972.

[91]

It would be absurd to suggest that there are no obstacles to be faced, especially for someone who wishes to advocate non-trendy heresies (such as opposition to the Race Relations Act) or a cause with little demagogic appeal but outside the gentleman's agreement regulating permitted partisan dispute (such as devaluation in 1964–67). Nevertheless, it can be done. In a 100 per cent socialist economy, the problem of finding an outlet becomes much more difficult. Heads of state publishing enterprises could be told to publish anything that will sell. But this is a very ambiguous instruction, and the fact that publishers are state employees must have some influence; and it is not open to anyone who disagrees with their verdict to set up on his own or find a private patron.

The argument is explained and developed at length in Professor Friedman's *Capitalism and Freedom*.[1] One of Friedman's most telling examples is of the victims of McCarthyite persecution, who found refuge in the private sector. The relevant point here is that political freedom depends on the existence of a large capitalist sector—a 'socialist market economy' will not do. A syndicalist society might be one better than a purely socialist one—the smaller the units in which 'workers' control' reigns the better from this point of view. But it is all too easy to imagine the syndicates exercising a common censorship. The refusal of the printers in a London evening newspaper to print an 'anti-union' cartoon was an ominous portent, and attempts have been made by members of NUJ chapels to bar opportunities to 'right wing' journalists.

These 'political' considerations point to the desirability not only of a 'private sector' with dispersed or institutional shareholders, but of some personal fortunes as well. Indeed, freedom of expression is probably stronger if the egalitarian 'correction' of the market distribution of wealth is not pushed too far. For although many controversial books and plays can be and are financed by publishers with institutional shareholders (who are small savers at one remove), the existence of wealthy patrons willing to go against the corporate philosophy (or artistic fashion) of the day is an important additional safeguard. (It made possible, for example, the launching of *Private Eye*.)

This 'political' argument can, however, easily be pushed too far, or in the wrong direction. It does not rule out the existence of a substantial state sector, nor give much guidance on how large it can safely be; nor does it help on many issues of economic policy which come up every day in a mixed company. Moreover, it can be persuasively argued that freedom of expression (and choice of types of employment, and many other things, too) will be

[1]University of Chicago Press, 1962.

[92]

strengthened if there are not merely a multiplicity of firms within the capitalist sector, but a multiplicity of *forms* of ownership— large private corporations, state-owned enterprises, one-man firms, producer and consumer co-operatives, and so on. This is particularly so where real or alleged technical factors limit the number of outlets, as in television. While a state broadcasting monopoly would be a monstrosity (one has only to recall how Churchill was prevented from speaking on the BBC before the Second World War), freedom of expression is almost certainly stronger as a result of the rivalry between the BBC and the independent channels than it would be if competition were confined to two or three private networks.

Moreover, the value of either private enterprise or of a multiplicity of forms of ownership for free expression depends on competition—not on perfect competition, but on the absence of formal or informal restrictive agreements. Friedman himself points to the Hollywood boycott of 'subversive' writers in the 1950s, possible only because of a collusive agreement among film-makers regulating who could be employed.

V. THE ROLE OF ECONOMICS—POSITIVE OR NORMATIVE?

The relation of the market economy to economics as an academic discipline is an elusive subject. A large number of economists are, of course, highly suspicious of the use of markets and prices. But they are exhibiting a reaction to a strong tradition within their own profession. Although they may think that they are opposing a pro-capitalist position, a little investigation soon shows that the actual policies of pro-capitalist governments bear very little relation to the doctrine of economic liberalism—indeed, Galbraith has taken a justified delight in explaining how President Nixon violated all its tenets. The *dirigistes* in the economics profession are ranged against a whole line of philosophically inclined economists from Adam Smith down to Hayek and Friedman rather than against a political party or a group of capitalists. Empirical evidence can be produced[1] to show that there is much more support for making use of the market in an advanced Western economy among economists than among politicians and commentators, and that economists of differing political beliefs often hold

[1] E.g. my *Is There an Economic Consensus?*, op. cit.

[93]

common policy positions which distinguish them from other educated laymen interested in public affairs.

This is a somewhat remarkable position for a would-be neutral science. It is related to a profound ambiguity about the subject matter of economics. According to one tradition (Marshall, Cannan, etc.) it is a science of human behaviour in relation to the material things of life, and therefore sheds light on the factors determining the growth of income and wealth. A different tradition (Robbins, drawing on Wicksteed and Walras) sees it as the science or logic of choice. According to the latter tradition, there is no such thing as economic ends. Economics is concerned with the allocation of resources, energy and time among alternatives, and the view of the economist as a philistine concerned to multiply material riches is itself a vulgar misconception.

There are usually deep-seated reasons why subjects do not fit nearly into logical pigeon-holes and the debate will not be resolved by proclaiming dogmatically that one or other concept is the right one. There is an inevitable strain between the two approaches, but they have co-existed (often within the same individual) for nearly a century and neither is likely to give way completely to the other. It is simplest, however, to start with the older view—which also corresponds to the layman's image—that economics is concerned with behaviour in relation to material things, particularly where money can be brought into the picture.

The competence of the economist

The economist has so far had very little to say on many of the most important determinants of output and living standards, in particular on science and technology and attitudes towards change and innovation. Technological matters are the concern of other specialists, and essays by economists on national attitudes and other psychological intangibles carry no more weight than those of anyone else. The main subject on which they can even aspire to a professional competence is the functioning of markets, and, in particular, the way in which supply and demand are related to prices and incomes. As we have already seen, the price mechanism, even when used for paternalist objectives, is a relatively *liberal means*.

Economics without price (and without markets)

In most individual markets *price* is the most important variable about which the economist can pronounce. Whether an economist is investigating the steel industry or the structure of fares, his contribution is likely to be mainly on pricing policy and the disaggregation of costs and receipts from different activities. It is only when it comes to the attempted macro-economic management of demand and output in the economy as a whole that an 'economics without price' (and without markets) has been evolved. 'Keynesian' fiscal policy, of the type practised for most of the post-war period, has attempted to control output entirely via real incomes, indeed, the associated forecasts and policy recommendations have been in 'real terms' and have largely abstracted from any influence of either absolute or relative prices. It is therefore not surprising that economists of the 'national income forecasting' school are less wedded to market-oriented attitudes than their colleagues (but also less keen on *detailed* market intervention, as they pin so much faith on *global* management). Even in their case, however, the role of price is forcibly brought home via the effect of the exchange rate on the external balance; and the competence of economists again lies in their analysis of front- or back-door exchange rate changes—which are of course a special kind of price. It does not lie in exhortations to export more, or in whipping up enthusiasm inside industrial committees such as the 'Little Neddies'.

Growth models in industrialised and developing countries

Another kind of economics which minimises markets or prices arises from growth models which make the proportion of the national income invested (especially in manufacturing industry) the key to growth and from this go on to suggest that the forcible reduction of the share of consumption in the national income (helped perhaps by overseas aid) is the key to prosperity.[1] This structure of ideas still has some influence in advanced industrial countries; but it always had too many weaknesses to become the main strand of economic thinking there. Differences in investment ratios were found to be inadequate to account for observed differences in growth rates; in any case, the investment differences seemed at least as likely to be a *consequence* as a *cause* of growth. Moreover, the idea of the capital market and the rate of interest as having some relevance to choice between present and future satisfactions never entirely lost hold; and the various distortions in the market allegedly keeping investment too low have been offset in recent thinking by the emphasis on environmental spill-over which might make it undesirably high. It is mainly in

[1][These concepts are examined critically by Douglas Rimmer, *Macromancy: The ideology of 'development economics'*, Hobart Paper 55, IEA, 1973.—ED.]

connection with developing countries and the Third World that economic explanations which play down prices and markets have really captured mainstream thinking.[1]

Indeed, economics, conceived as the study of behaviour affecting material wealth, has remarkably little to say on the effects of different political and economic systems and ideologies. There have been fast-growing economies in both the capitalist and the Communist world; and even among Western countries there has been almost no systematic relation between growth rates and degrees of intervention. It may be possible by forced draft methods, involving very undemocratic socialism, to increase a country's statistical growth rate, but the benefit of such methods to real living standards lies always somewhere in the future. No country relying on them has yet been seen to give its citizens a higher level of material prosperity than that prevailing in the US or North West Europe, even when judged by conventional indices.

Material wealth and choice

The obstinate question arises, however, how we should know if and when this overtaking has happened, and here is where the other concept of economics as the logic or science of choice inescapably obtrudes. Talk of material wealth or money incomes 'at constant prices' cannot hide the truth that that is no unique way of measuring the changes in a bundle of thousands of different sets of commodities and services, the composition of which is constantly changing. Money values can be used to add apples and pears only because, in a market system, relative prices are supposed to give some idea of individual preferences, choices and satisfactions. It is theoretically possible to reject consumer sovereignty and use some other basis of valuation; but in that event an alternative set of criteria has to be provided.

Economic efficiency is subjective

Some form of capitalist market economy is supported by many businessmen and politicians who clearly do not regard personal freedom and individual choice as the most important values. If asked for their reason they might well say that it promotes efficiency. It is quite irrational to seek to maximise *engineering efficiency* under almost any political or economic system. If the heat-energy conversion ratio of a machine can be raised from

[1]For reflections on this phenomenon, P. T. Bauer, *Dissent on Development,* Weidenfeld & Nicolson, 1972, and H. G. Johnson (ed.), *Economic Nationalism in Old and New States,* Allen & Unwin, 1968.

49 to 50 per cent by multiplying the cost ten-fold, it would be extremely wasteful to do this except under the most freakish conditions of labour supply and final product demand.

Economic efficiency is, however, a subjective criterion. A businessman asked to produce x units of a particular commodity will search around the available production methods and any new ones he can discover until there is no further change he can find which will reduce costs any more. He is 'maximising efficiency' from the point of view of his own self interest. (The exact efficiency conditions have long been given in books on economic principles, but were rediscovered in more complex mathematical form under such titles as 'operational research'.)[1]

But why should minimum costs for a firm be a sign of efficiency from any wider point of view? The price an employer offers for every marginal unit of labour, raw material and other inputs he buys has to be high enough to cover what that unit could produce in its next best employment, before he can succeed in bidding it away. The price paid by the employer therefore represents the alternatives foregone by society to produce an extra unit of the commodity in question.

But how are these alternatives valued? Let us suppose that the final addition to the labour force has come from a cheese factory and the producer we are discussing manufactures ice-cream. There is no *objective* way of valuing ice-cream in relation to cheese. It is efficient to pay enough to attract an extra worker from the cheese to the ice-cream factory if the person or body judging efficiency accepts consumers' relative valuation of marginal units of the two commodities. If he does not, and values cheese more highly, it might be inefficient to move this man to the ice-cream factory, even though the shift was the most profitable course of action open to the two manufacturers and the man himself.

Productive efficiency can, however, be given a meaning under paternalist value-judgements. Suppose that the government decided that the social value of cheese was much higher than the free market price. It would then subsidise the production of cheese, at so much per unit. The cheese manufacturer would then be able to offer higher wages; and it might not then pay the ice-cream manufacturer to bid away any more labour. Thus, entirely different quantities of output, and perhaps different methods of production, might become more efficient on the basis of a change in the methods of valuation of the two commodities. Alternatively, the government might ban ice-cream production as an undesirable

[1]E.g., in H. Townsend (ed.), *Price Theory,* Penguin Modern Economics Readings, 1971.

product. This is tantamount to a nil valuation of ice-cream; and in the changed labour market it might then pay the cheese manufacturer to take on more men and expand his output still further.

The notion of efficiency only has a meaning in connection with some pre-announced basis of valuation. If the government distrusts the consumer's judgement and announces neither a tax, nor a subsidy, nor a purchasing price of its own, but simply talks vaguely about the evils of ice-cream, the profit motive will not lead to an 'efficient' allocation of resources from the government's own point of view.

Value and value-judgements

It should *en passant* be noted that many of the most widely used criteria for assessing the worth of different kinds of output cannot derive from any value-judgements held by sane men. One can justify consumer valuation on liberal value-judgements; one can justify a zero price on drugs and a subsidy for milk from a paternalist desire to promote health. But there is no system of ethics which puts a special valuation on the balance of payments, or saving foreign exchange or promoting exports to preserve some arbitrary rate of exchange. Only those besotted with two or three decades of official half-truths could suppose otherwise. At most, on certain narrow, short-term nationalist assumptions, the UK can turn the terms of trade in its favour by exporting more, and importing less, than at a free trade exchange rate. This might justify limited levies on imports (or exports) if one is confident about the outcome of the ensuing trade war. It cannot conceivably support the view that exports or import-saving produce some special sort of value incommensurable with home output, and have to be promoted quite irrespective of return.

Markets, straitjackets, and the collapse of constraints

If we clear away these fallacies, the underlying logic of many Conservative supporters of the market economy (and of some others), who clearly do not accept an anti-paternalist or permissive society, is that the government should seek to influence the direction of national effort by a whole series of taxes, subsidies and bans; and, on the basis of these corrected valuations, market forces could then be allowed to encourage productive efficiency of those things which it is good for us to have.

The libertarian can, however, comfort himself with the knowledge that it is extremely difficult to put capitalism into a straitjacket of this kind. There is always an incentive to look for close substitutes for the banned or heavily taxed product, or to invent

[98]

entirely new goods and services not envisaged in the rule book of the moral censors. Moreover, differences of view among the establishment will frequently prevent very comprehensive systems of paternalist valuation on the lines suggested in the previous paragraph. The example of the Nazi war economy, cited earlier, is very much an exception and not the rule. The history of capitalist markets has been one of gradual collapse of the restraining walls of authority and convention, with the profit motive always one jump ahead of the Lord Chancellor and the Archbishops. The process could even be beginning in Japan where, until recently, capitalism worked within a very highly authoritarian and *dirigiste* general framework.

VI. BEYOND THE PURITAN ETHIC—THE ECONOMICS OF SELLING AND GIVING

Altruism and the market[1]

It is possible that the revulsion against the pursuit of ever-greater material wealth, recently characteristic of a few radical students (and also some upper- and middle-class traditionalists), is a portent of wider change. It is always worth examining the implication of developments at present visible only on a small scale and still untypical of the bulk of the population. Let us then suppose that there were a widespread weakening of the desire towards additional personal consumption. What would be the consequences?

Such a shift in outlook could come about in various ways. It is convenient to start off by assuming that it is part of a new ethical outlook, rather than a mere change of tastes. Both are of course involved in the movement towards the 'alternative society'; but the analysis of an ethical revulsion against selfishness is, in practice, less complicated than that of a shift of preferences from consumer goods towards other things. To make any progress at all, it is necessary to proceed in stages.

What, then, would follow from a belief that the search for maximum individual self-gratification is wrong, and from the desire to see a new order based on altruism rather than institutionalised 'selfishness'? General altruism is a concept capable of several interpretations. *First*, the most extreme form is the advocacy of complete unselfishness and total dedication to the welfare of others. This would be internally inconsistent if adopted

[1][Aspects of the economics of giving are discussed in IEA Readings No. 12, *The Economics of Charity*, 1974, where Professor David Johnson refers to 'the charity market'.—ED.]

[99]

as a general rule. The paradox of total unselfishness is that it is possible to be selfless only because some people are concerned with their own selfish desires or needs. If everybody were concerned with the welfare only of others, there would be nothing for altruists to do. A *second*, slightly less extreme form would be to love one's neighbour as much as—but not more than—oneself. A practitioner of such an ethic, carried to its logical conclusion, would devote his efforts to improving the welfare of the human race, or his fellow countrymen, and would be prepared to forego, for their benefit, any excess of his income above the general run. A *third* sort of altruistic ethic would allow modest material objectives, by definition less than the maximum obtainable, but forego any available excess for the sake of others.

Altruism and benevolence, if they are to be any other than individual eccentricities, presuppose a measure of self-regard; and novelists and psychologists have always known that those who despise themselves cannot love other people. Thus, we can confine our attention to the second and third varieties—an unwillingness to obtain for oneself more than either the generally available average, or some specified minimum, while there are others who are worse off. Various qualifications and permutations of these codes can be envisaged. An ethical inhibition against maximising one's own standard of living, present when the poorest are suffering from malnutrition, may, without any fundamental change of outlook, disappear if poverty comes to mean possessing only one car.

I am here not concerned with those who are prepared to make such penal sacrifices only if others do so as well. My concern is with the logical consequence of altruism as an individual ethic. An almost insuperable initial difficulty is deciding what is the correct reference group.[1] Is an altruist to forego personal riches to raise the standard of living of his neighbours, fellow countrymen, or of the entire human race?

It is difficult to find any convincing argument for limiting altruism to the frontiers of the nation-state—except for a pathological nationalist who has intense feelings of brotherhood for his fellow countrymen, but regards everyone else as a member of a different species. There seems no more reason for restricting benevolent and unselfish behaviour to the inhabitants of the UK than to the inhabitants of Greater London, or the enlarged EEC, or members of one's own profession. The conclusion would seem to be that the consistent altruist should want the benefit of any limitation on his own living standard devoted to the poorest inhabitants of the poorest countries.

[1]The 'successive circles of obligation' are discussed in pp. 113–114.

An altruist who felt that 'development aid' did more harm than good could subscribe to purely charitable relief organisations. Apart from worrying about the forms in which this help should be given, or its long-term effect, the altruist may despair at the smallness of the impact of his efforts, and those of like-minded people, if spread thinly over thousands of millions; and he may prefer to make a discernible impact on living standards nearer home, which he is also in a better position to assess for himself. But once he does this, he is conceding that he does not attach equal value to every human being; and he can have no tenable objection to the liberal-individualist ethic which attaches most weight to one's family and friends, somewhat lesser weight to professional colleagues or others with shared interests and outlook, and so on in ever-widening circles until the boundaries of the whole human race are reached.[1]

Maximising giving by maximising income

But however the altruist solves these conundrums, one general observation can be made. This is that there is little reason for him to refrain from maximising his own income. The difference between himself and other citizens, if he is logical, should be in what he does with his gains. Indeed, if anything, he should work beyond the point at which the self-centred citizen decides that the additional ('marginal') reward is not worth the additional ('marginal') effort, in order to increase the surplus he has available for charitable purposes. A society dominated by dedicated and consistent altruists would, therefore, be a pretty puritanical one, which is one of the reasons why I do not find the prospect attractive. Indeed, there have been resemblances to it among the frugal, hard-working, devout rising middle classes during several eras of economic advance. The main difference is that the wealth that was foregone in personal enjoyment was devoted only in small measure to improving the lot of other human beings, but was largely devoted to the 'higher' purposes of religion or further capital accumulation.

The important point, however, is that there is no reason why an altruist should not, within the limits indicated below, play to win. The presumption in favour of buying in the cheapest market and selling in the dearest, and gaining the best return on his talents, applies at least as much to him as to his self-oriented

[1]The implications of such a realistic weighting are discussed in my essay on 'Morality and Foreign Policy', in *Capitalism and the Permissive Society*, pp. 337-40.

colleagues. A business man does not serve his fellows, least of all the poorest of them, by selling a product at a minimal profit well below that which the market will bear.

Selective and indiscriminate giving

If he were to do so, the most likely result would be a misallocation of scarce resources, which is likely to make the community worse off; and there is no presumption that the poor will escape the effects. Even the apparent direct transfer from his own pocket to others by holding his prices down below the market level will be misdirected, as a large part of the gain will inevitably flow to those who are, by altruistic lights, undeserving of his largesse. He would be better advised to behave in a normal commercial manner and use the larger sum then at his disposal for redistribution according to his own philanthropic principles.[1]

This advice, is of course, only an approximation to the truth, due to the imperfections of economic policy. Although it would be best if the state were to lay down rules of the game and adjust its taxes and subsidies so that the pursuit of self-interest also promoted the general prosperity, we know that a market economy will never, in practice, be managed with ideal wisdom. Firms are not always made to pay for the overspill costs that their waste products or their heavy trucks impose on the community. Workers displaced by technological or other change may not be reabsorbed into other jobs—whether because of mistaken official financial policies, or the monopolistic activities of trade unions. Undesirable changes in the distribution of income caused, say, by a rise in basic food prices, are best corrected via the tax and social security system; but we cannot always rely on the correction being made.

Thus, playing the market game must always be tempered by common sense; and this applies not merely to the declared altruist, but also the ordinary humane citizen. The absence of a law making me pay full compensation for all the foul products my factory pours into a river does not give me a moral licence to go on polluting (although I may be under financial pressures to do so). There is no general politico-economic outlook that can excuse inflicting specific harm on others, especially identifiable individual human beings in a weaker position, without attempt at redress. The takeover king who shows the faithful servant of the old firm the door, without asking what is to become of him, is not a good Manchester liberal but a callous malefactor.

[1]Efficiency in giving is discussed *inter alia* by several authors in *The Economics of Charity, op. cit.*

These qualifications do not destroy the general presumption against subordinating the profit motive to some supposedly higher ideal. A businessman, however altruistic, should be very careful before reducing his rate of return for some abstract goal, such as 'lower prices', 'an incomes policy', 'the export drive', or 'the need to invest'. He is not professionally qualified to calculate the remoter consequences of a supposedly patriotic deviation from the pursuit of his interest. Nor, in all probability, are those who provide these exhortations. Moreover, even when it comes to avoiding specific harm to known individuals, an altruistic or humanitarian employer would be better advised to concentrate on such matters as the early spotting of redundancies and making personal efforts to retrain and find other jobs for those displaced, rather than attempt to maintain an inflated work-force, or to 'buy British' when the foreign product gives better value. Of course, painful dilemmas cannot always be avoided in this way; but the sensible humanitarian will try to minimise them by intelligent planning of *his own* activities rather than by taking pride in the smallness or even the 'reasonableness' of his profits.

Rejection of material consumption

An altruist of the kind described may be very fond of consumer goods and simply think it wrong to have more of them than his less fortunate neighbours. It is, however, useful to extend the analysis from altruism to a more general rejection of the striving for ever-increasing amounts of goods and services as a false goal.

It is possible that the existence of a minority of people, who had already undergone such a change in tastes, and preferred idleness or social security benefit to the extra material gain available from work, may have had something to do with the much higher 'unemployment' figures in the early 1970s than in previous cyclical peaks.[1] But, in default of worthwhile evidence, I should be surprised if this is more than a part of the explanation. In any event, whatever may have been the motivation of the non-employed, there is not the slightest reason to suppose that the saturation of consumer wants is the reason for the difficulties that have occurred in recent years in maintaining 'effective demand' at previously customary levels. The anti-consumption values under

---

[1] J. B. Wood, *How Much Unemployment?*, Research Monograph 28, IEA, 1972, dissects the total of official unemployment into different elements; see also my *Second Thoughts on Full Employment Policy*, Centre for Policy Studies, 1975.

discussion are still shared by a minority. Most people could still find plenty on which to spend extra income.

Tastes and behaviour are not, however, immutable; and it is worth asking whether a revulsion from any further increase in material consumption—feelings at present confined to minority groups—would be compatible with a competitive market economy. However strong the historical connection between the rise of capitalist markets (or earlier mercantile systems) and materialistic preoccupations, need this connection hold good in the future? This question is best investigated by treating the revulsion from the pursuit of ever more goods and services as a pure change of taste in a society that has already reached an advanced level of technology and is capable of producing a Gross National Product that is, by historical standards, high.

The simplest case to envisage is that the majority of the population become satisfied with a lower level of material reward, in the form of either private or collective consumption, than they could obtain from the earnings of a working week of the present customary length. The higher the general level of hourly real wages (in other words, the more successful 'the system' has been in the past), the more such people there are likely to be; and the less heroic, or ascetic, they will need to be to sustain such an attitude. Let us at this stage assume that they can fill extra leisure hours to their own satisfaction.

A competitive system based on market forces is surely likely to prove most satisfactory to such 'non-consumers'. For a profit-making businessman is not interested in the private values of his workers. If they wish to work fewer hours for less money, or only one week in four, that is their affair. If irregular and unpredictable working habits impose difficulties in keeping up a smooth flow of production, the rate for the job will be *pro rata* less than for workers willing to work in a more regular way. Indeed, as soon as it becomes apparent that there is a pool of potential workers available, who will be easier to recruit or require to be paid less provided they can work in amounts, and/or at times, of their own choosing, it will pay businessmen to adapt their production methods to such preferences; and those who do adapt themselves in this way will be able to undercut those who insist too rigidly on traditional working practices.[1]

[1] Timing systems to enable companies to offer flexible work hours or 'flextime' have been marketed commercially. One of the pioneers was Messerschmidt in Germany; and after *The Financial Times* described the introduction of such a system into Pilkington Laboratories (18 April, 1972), it was 'bombarded' with inquiries. By the beginning of 1974 about 500 organisations employing some 100,000 workers had adopted such arrangements, according to a report by the Unit for Manpower Studies (*Department of Employment Gazette*, January 1975).

The difficulties in the way of the 'alternative' culture come from the monopolistic and anti-capitalist element of our society. This would be readily admitted in the case of restrictive practices by businessmen who agree not to undercut each other with irregular labour. But the largest obstacles arise from union monopolies, which insist on fixing wages and conditions by collective agreements that do not easily permit variations to suit minority preferences. It would not take long for the shop stewards to 'call everyone out' if an employer were to be found taking on individual workers at below the regular rate in return for an unusual and costly pattern of working hours or a toleration of absenteeism. (The systems of flexible time-keeping now being introduced experimentally are presumably not very costly—they may even be beneficial—for company efficiency.) The point would be blindingly obvious were it not for the traditional association between being on the 'left' and having pro-union sympathies. It is no coincidence that the occupations suggested in that excellent publication *Alternative London*,[1] which range from interviewing for market surveys and selling charter flights, to minicab driving, 'busking', window cleaning and working in bistros, are the least unionised of activities. Nevertheless, if the preference for leisure, or irregular work, over take-home pay became sufficiently widespread, even union negotiators would be forced to give it attention.

An interesting corroboration of this line of argument is the degree of toleration of people who 'opt out' in various countries. It is most common in countries with vestigial attachment to competitive capitalism such as the US and the UK; it is least in the centrally-planned Communist societies, while in countries with a tradition of state-regulated capitalism and a dislike of market forces, such as France, the position is midway between the two.

If the distaste for accumulation of goods and services came to be predominant, competition would, of course, change its nature. There might still be a good deal of investment and entrepreneurial action if consumer desires, although modest, were subject to frequent alterations of taste; the 'gear' that is fashionable might be subject to frequent change, or trips to old coal-mines might alternate with visits to Kabul, or painting one's home in a novel manner, as ways of spending leisure.

The need for such continuing investment would reduce social welfare as conventionally defined by economists. For people would have to sacrifice some leisure, or work a little less irregularly, or

[1] N. Saunders, *Alternative London* (Saunders/Wildwood House, 4th edn., 1974).

make do with fewer goods and services to leave aside a margin for this investment. But it could well be argued that it is only such changes of tastes and fashion that would prevent the envisaged society from becoming utterly stagnant. It is a defect of the treatment of changes of tastes by writers on welfare economics that they are seen only as wasteful reductions in the standard of living.

Static consumption and population

Purely for the sake of analysis, let us, nevertheless, assume that consumer requirements are not merely modest but static, and that there is no population growth. *Provided the transition from the present pattern to this situation is sufficiently gradual,* there is no reason to predict general bankruptcies, the collapse of capitalism, or that it would be impossible for any other reason to give effect to the new pattern of static tastes and desires.

As the growth of consumer demand declines during the transitional period, we should expect that net investment would eventually drop to zero. The rate of return on capital and the real rate of interest would fall off. The situation would be similar to what Keynes had in mind when he spoke of the euthanasia of the *rentier*. Owing to the fall in the rate of return, the share of interest and profit in the national income could be expected to fall drastically over time. Whatever profits there were would largely be distributed, as there would be no scope for reinvestment. Where, however, as in small businesses, profits were a substitute for managerial salaries, market forces would keep them in existence.

Keynes and the 10-hour week society

The stock of fixed-interest securities (including deadweight national debt) would not yield any more real income (unless prices fell); but their capital value and the wealth of their owners would rise several-fold as interest rates dropped, and this would tend to counteract the other forces reducing the inequality of wealth. The owners of these securities could work even less than the rest of the community—assuming that they, too, did not desire more material goods. But the effect on the welfare of everyone else would, in these circumstances, be trivial. If 90 per cent of the population worked ten hours a week and 10 per cent with fixed-interest securities now had to work an average of only one hour, the loss to the 90 per cent from the existence of this private wealth would be one hour more work per week than would be otherwise necessary. If even this is regarded as unacceptable, the wealth effect on fixed-interest owners could be counteracted by a moderate annual capital levy.

Mention of Keynes is very appropriate in this context. For the kind of situation here discussed is one in which there could well be involuntary unemployment, in the sense that, in the absence of appropriate policies, effective demand for goods and services might not be sufficient to employ people even for the limited number of hours for which they were prepared to work. Involuntary unemployment, if it occurred, could be cured in this situation by some combination of monetary expansion and budgetary deficits.

Nor is there anything that need be incomprehensible to the layman in these remedies. All one has to do is to imagine everyone in our 10-hour a week 'non-consuming' society receiving a cash sum through the post. Either he would spend slightly more or (if the static-wants hypothesis is taken literally) he would want to work less, or some combination of the two would occur. The demand for labour would rise and the supply would fall off, until there was eventually no more involuntary unemployment.

Function of money and markets

It is worth listing the advantages of maintaining a monetary economy based on the market even in our hypothetical society where consumer wants are very modest in relation to potential output, and have ceased to grow. Obviously a capitalist market economy would, in such circumstances, be a very different animal from anything we now know. The capital goods sector would be very much smaller, as it would be concerned only with replacement and not with expansion or modernisation. Entrepreneurial or technological ability would command a smaller market price; and parts of business, and perhaps government, would become a routine. The society would, in some ways, resemble the mercantile economy that existed before the Industrial Revolution or the more stagnant economies of the West such as Spain or Ireland until a couple of decades ago—with the all-important difference that there would be no involuntary poverty or unemployment to disfigure it.

It is important to note that, in this type of economy, consumer wants would be *static* but not *satiated*. There could be no satiation of wants while labour still had a 'marginal disutility'—in other words, while people still regarded work as something they would rather not do, or would rather do less of, were it not for the need to earn a living. For if wants were literally satiated, but the last hour of work still carried a disutility, it would pay people to reduce their hours of work and their earnings until goods reacquired some utility at the margin. The assumption of static wants implies that people would seek to enjoy the benefits of technological progress entirely in the form of reduced hours of work and not at all in increased take-home pay.

The retention of money payments in this static economy would allow people to choose their preferred combination of goods and services, which would not be possible if consumption were organised collectively; and, most important, people would be able to retain choice of employment. Production would be organised as efficiently as possible—which, in this situation, means that given wants could be supplied with the minimum of work hours. For, if a more efficient method were anywhere available, profits would ensue for a temporary period to anyone who utilised them—although they would eventually be eroded by competition and the system return to its static state.

Above all, no one would be forced to conform to a single life style. People who did not share the prevailing anti-consumption, anti-work ethos could 'opt into' the consumer society without disturbing their neighbours; and there could still be luxury hotels or ocean cruises for those who wanted them and were prepared to work to obtain them. At the other extreme, those who were prepared to sacrifice even more monetary income than the majority—in return for, say, a five-hour week or highly irregular work—could do so. Indeed, it will have struck the economist reader that the traditional theoretical arguments that competitive markets (subject to certain well known exceptions and necessary corrective devices) produce a 'social optimum' come into their own in the static condition we have been describing—although the result will not look much like capitalism as we know it.

The claim that a less consumption-orientated society could not hope to come into existence, because capitalism would smother it, mostly boils down, on examination, to the grossly inflated view of the powers of advertising (discussed in pp. 54–56). Clearly the business community has a vested interest in maintaining at least some economic growth, but its political power to distort choice in this direction almost invariably springs from *interventionist* economic policies designed to prop up unprofitable enterprises in the name of technology, nationalism or a *simpliste* interpretation of full employment.[1]

---

[1] A bias in favour of intervention is one of the unfortunate heritages bequeathed by the Old Left to the New. Unfortunately, the extensive and indefensible rigging of the market by political authorities to favour particular interest groups is not the only reason why the opponents of the consumer society feel that the dice are loaded against them. Indeed, if anything, their bias is in favour of such intervention as a matter of principle. Their real difficulty may be that most people do not as yet share their tastes; and toleration of people with different tastes is not always the hallmark of those who talk most about 'liberation' and 'freedom'.

Surplus goods, scarce work

One can readily imagine a situation in which some goods are no longer scarce and some types of work are. Some goods are even now so cheap that people of average income can be indifferent to how much of it they spend on them. There are already all kinds of work—known as hobbies—which people will *pay* to do. (Standing for Parliament would thus count for some as a hobby.) While for the most part people pay in money (i.e. foregone goods) for their hobbies, this is not entirely so. People pay for one type of hobby in the opportunities foregone for pursuing another. Members of the establishment pay for sitting on the marginal committee by not being able to sit on yet another on which they place a slightly lower valuation; and they would forego many hours on minor advisory groups for the sake of far fewer hours on a really prestigious Royal Commission. We are already moving towards a situation in which many kinds of work have a positive utility; to the extent that market prices prevail, they will have a cost not merely in commodities foregone, but in terms of other kinds of pleasurable work.

'Non-economic' goods

On the goods side, a growing number of commodities can be expected to enter a category which, for want of a better label, I shall call 'non-economic'. My definition of a non-economic commodity is one for which the demand is no longer responsive to *relative* prices. In other words, the person or group of people under consideration will not shift to substitutes, and will buy the same amount whatever happens to its price *relative to other prices*. Of course, a rise in the price of any commodity will itself reduce the real value of any given income. To allow for this factor, we shall assume that *real* incomes are constant and that a compensating financial sum is paid in such cases to make them so. This is not, of course, a policy proposal, but simply a way of defining 'other things being equal'.[1] (We are thus defining a non-economic good as one for which the pure substitution elasticity of demand is zero.) The smaller the proportion of income going on a commodity, the less important is this definitional complication.

'Free' goods

It should be noted that a non-economic good is not the same as a 'free' good in the usual sense of a commodity that is not in scarce supply, i.e. each member of the community can have as much of it as he likes without anyone else having to sacrifice any

[1] This is indeed Professor Friedman's interpretation of the ordinary demand curve: *Essays in Positive Economics,* Chicago, 1953.

other desired commodity. Thus, fresh air in an uncontaminated rural area would have a zero cost in foregone alternatives. Bread might come into the category of a non-economic good, if demand were invariant to price. But it would not be a free good, because farming, milling and baking would take up scarce resources, which could be used to produce alternative goods that the community has now to do without.

My definition of a non-economic good is, however, very close to the usual definition of a 'necessity'; I suspect, however, that there are few necessities the demand for which is literally unresponsive to relative prices. It is a reasonable guess—although no more than that—that, as a community grows wealthier, more and more goods enter the truly non-economic category. There is, of course, always the question: non-scarce for whom? A starving man with a few pence in his pocket will take into account relative prices very carefully before he decides what to buy. Indifference to price for a growing number of commodities is only a reasonable guess even for the future, if it is assumed that a minimum level of personal income is maintained by state action, and that this minimum itself grows in line with general prosperity.

The opponents of the price mechanism and the monetary economy have a strong case in relation to such non-economic goods, and *only* in relation to them. For, if the quantity sold has no relation to price, the function of prices in helping to allocate consumers' expenditure in line with their preferences disappears. So equally does the function of prices and profitability in allocating production between alternative activities. The whole business of taking money, with all its distributional, clerical and policing problems, is thus a costly waste; and the state might as well purchase, in a block order, the quantities required by the public at a price just sufficient to make it worth the while of the supplying firms, and allow people to take as much as they like 'for free' in any convenient way. In this manner, the role of money and prices can be reduced in all those areas of our lives where they are not worth the bother, while retaining them in all the remaining areas in which they are still a vital instrument for combining free consumer choice with efficient use of resources.

Several traps have to be avoided if this proposal is not to do more harm than good. First, the identification of non-economic commodities is not nearly as obvious as it may seem. For example, domestic consumer demand for salt may be invariant to price, but not industrial demand. It would be very difficult to have free salt for housewives and restaurants only, while a general supply of free salt could lead to an irrational choice of production process in the chemical and other industries.

Secondly, and even more important, it is essential that *a state distribution system for 'free' products should not be given any sort of monopoly whatever*. For example, if bread were free, there might still be all sorts of *varieties*, not supplied by the state authorities, for which people would still be willing to pay. In addition, the number, location, or opening hours of distribution outlets for free bread may not suit some people. The only way to ascertain whether there are needs or desires left unsatisfied by the state scheme is to allow people to make a profit by trying to do better. Without this safeguard, the above proposal will only bring comfort to the enemies of personal choice and the friends of enforced uniformity.

A guarantee of minimum income/reverse income tax

The *assumption* of a minimum income rising with the general level of prosperity was made simply to help with a matter of definition. But I should now like to make it a definite proposal. What I have in mind is *not* statutory minimum wages, which have caused involuntary unemployment wherever they have been introduced, but social security payments to guarantee a certain cash flow related to family size.[1] They would have to be well below the average or median wage if they were not to be ruled out on 'incentive' grounds. But in an affluent society they could still provide a standard of living far above subsistence. This proposal cuts out the whole argument about 'scroungers and shirkers' by giving up the vain attempt to hunt them down. The potential shirker would be told in effect: 'The community is now rich enough to give you two choices: You can "opt out" if you wish and you will receive an allowance, which will be far from princely and well below the normal wage, but will allow you to live, and will also rise as the nation becomes richer; or you can work and go after much larger material prizes.'

The feasibility of the scheme depends partly on the empirical question of the size of the loss (arising out of the disincentive effect of a 100 per cent marginal rate of tax) from providing guaranteed subsistence to that portion of the population who have skills of relatively low market value, or who are the most work-shy.

At the beginning of 1970 four IEA co-authors[2] proposed a

[1]Cf. the discussion of the distribution of income in the early pages (pp. 57–60).

[2]Anthony Christopher (then Assistant Secretary, now General Secretary Designate, of the Inland Revenue Staff Federation), George Polanyi (Research Fellow, IEA), Arthur Seldon (Editorial Director, IEA), and Barbara Shenfield (formerly of the University of Birmingham and Bedford College, London).

scheme for a Minimum Income Guarantee that would make up to the Supplementary Benefit level all incomes at present below.[1] Of the 3 million householders that were expected to benefit, some 2¼ million were headed by retired people. The disincentive to extra effort from the 100 per cent marginal rate would thus have applied to some ¾ million people—mostly workers with large families whose earnings were below the Supplementary Benefits minimum.

The real problem, of course, was whether the unconditional guarantee of such a minimum as a 'right' would be prohibitively costly in terms of the number of people stopping work altogether and settling for this minimum. Policy here has been too long dominated by the spectre of Speenhamland, the late-18th-century system under which magistrates made up to minimum levels the wages of farm labourers. This led to large-scale resort to public assistance in preference to work. The reaction of Parliament was the notorious Poor Law of 1834, which confined relief to people entering 'indoor institutions' on very rigorous conditions.

The counter-argument of the IEA group was that such effects were to be expected at a time when the normal wage was no higher than the subsistence minimum. In 1970, probably no more than 2–3 per cent of the full-time occupied population had incomes below the suggested guarantee. The majority of workers would take a large cut of income if they chose to live on State benefit.

Thus, with present attitudes towards material goods, the cost of a modest income guarantee would be small; and only a limited number of people might take advantage of it. A combination of changing attitudes and the effects of increasing prosperity in raising the level of the guarantee would lead to more people taking advantage of it in the future. But then the very same factors would reduce the burden that the provision of this minimum imposed on those who prefer to work for a living.

In the IEA group scheme, the minimum income guarantee would be given in the form of a reverse income tax. Poor people who worked would thus not receive the full guaranteed minimum, but only the amount by which their actual earnings fell short of this minimum. While the scheme was at this stage, snooping and inspection would be necessary to check on undeclared earnings.

I would hope, however, that this would be only an intermediate stage and that eventually we would be prosperous enough to pay out the guaranteed minimum as a 'social dividend' irrespective of income from other sources. When that happened the whole in-

[1]*Policy for Poverty* (the Report of an IEA Study Group), Research Monograph 20, IEA, 1970.

vigilatory aspect of social security could come to an end—both the feelings of humiliation at the receiving end and the feelings of being duped on the part of the working taxpayer.

Markets without the puritan ethic

An attempt has been made in the last few pages to show that a market economy is not incompatible with the anti-commercial ethos of certain radicals, whose best elements it can reflect. The aspirations of those who wish to opt out of a work-oriented monetary economy are respected and acknowledged by the option of a modest but rising minimum payment, irrespective of effort. In addition a limited but growing number of standard goods and services could be provided without cash payment. This latter aspect will free even the more conventional of us from petty and irritating financial transactions, where there is a real utility loss in attempting too virtuously to maximise utility. Thus, the market economy can be gradually divorced from the puritan ethic.

But in return for these changes the apostles of the 'alternative society' must be prepared to recognise the activities of the remainder of the community who have aspirations for things which are still scarce—whether fur coats, Georgian houses, or visits to baroque churches—and who wish to continue to take part in a monetary economy. The faster the general advance of prosperity, the earlier these choices between different life styles will become a reality; and anti-growth propaganda only serves to prolong our present materialist and envious ethic.

There is a deal to argue about in the above proposals on figures and details. Orthodox opinion may legitimately query my suggestions on grounds of *present* cost; but if it rules out minimum incomes for the work-shy, or zero prices for non-economic goods, on grounds of *principle, irrespective of the level of affluence*, then it, too, is motivated by that moralistic resentment of other people's well-being which it decries in the egalitarians. We should not be influenced by the pain arising from intolerance of other people's enjoyment, from whatever side of the political spectrum this intolerance comes.

VII. CONCLUDING NOTES

Self-interest and the public interest

Most people acknowledge in their practical conduct successive circles of obligation, which are strongest towards those who are personally closest to them, somewhat less strong to those with whom they have national racial, religious or cultural affinities, and weakest of all towards the human race in general. A frank recognition of these successive rankings would be preferable—and lead to more humane results—than the customary proclamation of universal benevolence as the ideal to which all should aspire.

The real difficulty of this concept is not that it is reprehensible, but that it is related to a private code of morality in which the weights will differ from person to person, and is therefore not easy to translate into a set of public rules on which all, or most, can agree. For this purpose some impartial guide such as Rawls's 'veil of ignorance',[1] in which we ask ourselves what criteria we would accept if we did not know what our own particular station in society was to be, is clearly more suitable. But it still leaves open the question of the reference group; that is, of the exact society in which we are to imagine ourselves to be ignorant of our station. It is far from obvious that this should be the whole human race. The idea of a weighting system in which we attach smaller, but non-zero, weights to people outside our own country seems to me a helpful one for traditional types of foreign policy questions. It may even give us some clue in our present confused situation where there is strong and emotional disagreement about the relative degrees of obligation to British subjects, fellow members of the EEC and members of the Commonwealth of varying degrees of 'kinship'. But I can scarcely claim to have scratched the surface of the whole question of 'reference groups' which is one of the most neglected areas of both moral philosophy and of empirical political analysis.

Beliefs—reasons and validity

The *reasons* why people hold certain beliefs have no bearing on their *validity;* to suppose otherwise would be to fall into the same intellectual trap as the worst Marxist or Freudian camp followers (it is not a trap that Marx and, above all, Freud would have been guilty of themselves). Examination of the roots of widely-held views can, all the same, be useful in explaining why people persist in holding them, despite rational arguments to the contrary, and why the arguments fail to make a sufficient impression.

Among the middle classes and the establishment generally, adherence to competitive capitalism is, even where it exists, largely a matter of lip-service. Most middle-class voters who are not

[1]The concept of a 'veil of ignorance' is discussed in John Rawls, *A Theory of Justice*, Oxford University Press, 1972. Many of the principles which Professor Rawls derives with its aid are highly disputable; but the concept itself is very instructive.

business leaders hardly ever mention competitive capitalism, or any of its synonyms, except as dirty words. 'Less government' is a popular cry, not to promote freedom of any sort, but because those who utter it believe that it would lead to a transfer of income from other classes to themselves. 'Competitive capitalism' is not a partisan slogan. When it comes to the test of practical application, it has at least as many opponents among Conservative as among Labour supporters, and among businessmen as among trade unionists.

The support for capitalism of leading figures of industry, commerce and finance is rarely part of any wider libertarian outlook. Such people are not notable for their championship of libertarian causes outside the economic field. Prominent businessmen have the views that one would very much expect on 'permissiveness', the indiscipline of modern youth, drugs, the prosecution of obscene publications, and so on.

Even in their own professional sphere, the devotion of many in the business community to the competitive aspects of capitalism is usually conspicuous by its absence. While they may proclaim the virtues of competition in the abstract, their own industry is very often a special case qualifying for protective restriction, subsidy or regulation; and the organised leaders of business are often in the forefront of the drive for Government intervention, provided their own financial interests do not appear to suffer (and sometimes even when they do, such is the failure of nerve).

To come down to a slightly more technical level: the minority among the intellectual classes who bother to read the standard defences of capitalism by writers such as Friedman or Hayek soon find that the contemporary business leader not merely has seldom heard of the key propositions emphasised by them: the rule of impersonal law, consumer sovereignty and the separation of politics from business. On the contrary, his ideal is often that of negotiated deals with government officials on a 'power game basis' for projects for which the consumer would not be willing to pay and which have negative 'spillover' effects.

None of this is any cause for surprise and was long ago described by Adam Smith. The typical businessman is, after all, more often an administrator or manager than an entrepreneur. The virtues of *capitalism* have little to do with the intentions of *capitalists* who often frustrate, confound or weaken it, and, if there is far more competition in the longer run than the more *simpliste* critics suppose, it is because of the difficulty of keeping out new entrants, products and ideas, rather than because of any lack of desire to do so.

[115]

The logic of the system makes the capitalist a two-faced animal. When he faces outward in his business life he is, whether he likes it or not, in a permissive society. However much he spends on advertising, he must in the end persuade people to take his wares; and however much he dislikes the process, he must either influence or serve the public taste; he cannot use the weapon of coercion or the sanctity of tradition. Indeed, much of the business history of the post-war period consists of the replacement of the long-established Anglo-Saxon upper-middle-class managerial dynasties by immigrants or newcomers of 'non-U' stock, who had no fastidious scruples about catering for the requirements of a more affluent working class.

Although he operates within a libertarian framework in his outside dealings, and he must also have some regard to the preferences of his work-force in conditions of high employment, within his organisation the capitalist manager operates by authority and not via commercial forces. Within the wider community the business executive is on the side of authority, he identifies himself with the governors rather than the governed and expects their support in his difficulties, and seems to have more in common with unambiguous authority figures such as judges, senior civil servants, generals, or headmasters than with the representatives of permissive culture, whether pop stars or 'trendy left' journalists. Yet, in his own business life, especially if he is a successful innovator, he is engaged in undermining accepted ways and destroying established values and practices. He is sandwiched between two worlds. He cannot identify himself with radical protest or with anti-authoritarian sentiment of any kind, for he realises that these forces, if unleashed, would sweep away his own position.

Capitalism and rationality

Capitalist civilisation is above all rationalist. It is anti-heroic and anti-mystical. The spirit that animates it is the very opposite of 'Theirs not to reason why, theirs but to do or die'. The successful capitalist is forced by circumstances to query the way everything is done and endeavour to try and find a better way. If he relies on a traditional, mystical or ceremonial justification of existing practices, he will be overtaken by someone else and may well sink into oblivion. The breakdown of theological authority, the rise of the scientific spirit and the growth of capitalism were interrelated phenomena. A new ethic arose in the 17th century and had grown to fruition by the 19th, which blessed empirical and logical inquiry, denigrated the claims of authority and legitimised the profit motive (*inter alia* by removing the mediæval restraints on usury and the notion of the 'just price').

So long as the capitalist and the scientific segments were contained within an essentially aristocratic order, which preserved many traditions, superstitions and entrenched customs and, above all, deferential attitude towards a traditional ruling class—as was the case throughout most of the 19th century—capitalism could flourish. But in time the sceptical inquiring attitude was bound to turn on established institutions, and not only on kings or the restricted franchise, but on capitalism itself.

Understanding the price mechanism

Unfortunately, a refusal to take on trust the customs and institutions of society (which is the negative part of the rational critique) does not itself bring a willingness to accept or understand rational arguments. It requires an intellectual and imaginative effort to understand the allocative function of the price mechanism, to see how a high (relative) price will set in motion forces that will remedy a shortage, how the shift of workers from bankrupt to expanding enterprises can increase prosperity, and eventually benefit even the workers who are transferred. Above all, it takes considerable insight or powers of analysis—and a rare freedom from envy—to see the *harmful* implications of paying people according to presumed merit rather than market values, or to see the advantages as well as disadvantages of the private ownership of capital and the dangers of simply trying to suppress it.

The dilemma of the economic liberal

The economic libertarian, who recognises the strengths of some aspects of capitalism, has to face many drawbacks. Unless he is an apologist for business interests, or a party politician, he is bound to be highly critical of the particular forms of capitalism which prevail and of the policies of Conservative and Republican Governments. To them he will appear as a far-out radical or, at best, an impractical theorist. Yet, among students and the communication media which act as the middlemen for ideas, he will appear as a timid apologist for the 'system'.

Businessmen can usually be relied upon to defend the indefensible aspects of their activities while giving in to their collectivist opponents on all essentials. Nor is this a criticism; businessmen are paid to *operate* the system rather than to understand or expound it. Nothing is more pathetic than to see politicians of either party coming cap in hand to industrialists or bankers for advice they are not qualified to give.

[117]

The question of the role of capitalism and state enterprise has brought to light several different traditions among supporters of the market economy. There is the *static* emphasis on supplying a given set of goods and services by known technology. From this point of view a competitive market economy will bring about an optimum solution, subject to well-known exceptions, which in turn have well-known remedies found in standard texts. To emphasise the general rule is to be a 'market economist'; to emphasise the exceptions and remedies is to be described as a 'planner' of sorts. The ideal can be regarded as a market economy with numerous corrective interventions, or a regulated economy making considerable use of prices and market forces.

Another type of approach is more *dynamic*. It puts the emphasis on the role of market forces in stimulating new tastes and new methods of meeting both old and existing tastes. The danger of this approach is that it can be vulgarised into an abrasive outlook which takes positive delight in 'shaking people up'. This is, however, a distortion. There is nothing in the logic of the dynamic case for a market economy which causes the economist to regard a quiet, sleepy country with a low measured growth of GNP as inferior to a thrusting industrial state. All that is implied is that there must be freedom in both countries to innovate or carry on propaganda. If, in the first country, people are unresponsive to sales appeals (other than quietist or ascetic gospels) and do not take to new technology, there is no warrant for condemning that country and putting it lower in some absurd league table.

The conclusion needs, however, to be carefully stated. A country may have rising expectations and people may be prepared to change their habits to meet them; but growth may be held down because the country may have the misfortune to have a deficient supply of entrepreneurial talent (due perhaps to the educational system), or that talent may be discouraged by misguided taxation policies, or irrational official devotion to an arbitrary exchange rate or to the maintenance of a reserve currency role leading to 'stop–go' demand management policies, or for numerous other reasons. This was the element of truth in the 'growthmanship' of the 1960s; but it was hopelessly confused by many of its supporters and its opponents with the illiberal value-judgement that amenity should be sacrificed *without limit* for the sake of industrial production.

The following Table attempts to sub-divide economists who would use markets and prices according to the degree of *state intervention* associated with such use.

Preference for markets and prices as planning instruments	Preference for markets, with presumption against intervention
Strongly redistributive taxes and benefits	Acceptance of income and property distribution that emerges from the market
No special concern with ownership	Strong insistence on private enterprise
Sensitivity to differences between private and social costs, and readiness to intervene to reduce them	Readiness to intervene where large, clear and proven discrepancies between private and social costs, but benefit of doubt to non-interference
Onus on those responsible for change to compensate victims.	Change desirable if losers cannot 'bribe' those responsible to desist.

Those at the interventionist end of the spectrum would use what is here termed a corrected market economy, with special emphasis on the corrections. They have no particular interest in the pattern of ownership, but put great weight on redistribution via taxation and social service payments. This will do almost as well as a description of certain kinds of social democrat, although it will unfortunately not quite do as a description of even the 'Gaitskellite' wing of the British Labour Party. The anti-interventionist market economist, on the other hand, has clear affinities with certain strands of Conservative (although not Tory) thought.

These remarks apply to economists who come down consistently on one or other side of the Table. But there is no necessary relation between attitudes in the different sub-divisions. One can, for instance, be highly sensitive to environmental damage and not in the least willing to give the benefit of the doubt to the uncorrected market, yet be an out-and-out inegalitarian. Yet both schools of thought illustrated in the Table show a far better appreciation of the role of market incentives and prices than most politicians and opinion-formers in all political parties.

QUESTIONS FOR DISCUSSION

1. Define 'a market' and differentiate forms of markets in goods, labour, capital, land and money.

2. What are the main technical functions of markets? How are these functions performed in economies that attempt to dispense with markets?

3. 'Markets give bad results because incomes are unequal.' Do you agree? Give reasons for and against.

4. 'Markets yield inefficient use of resources because they ignore external costs and benefits.' Comment, with illustrations of market and non-market controls of external detriments such as pollution, congestion and destruction of natural beauty.

5. '... Savings decisions are made by mortal man whereas a "society" must conceive itself to be perpetual.' (Professor Joan Robinson, 1964.) Discuss this characteristic of the capital market. Is it necessarily a condemnation? How could capital markets be adapted to take account of longer time-horizons?

6. Would you argue that markets are effective/desirable for consumer goods but not for welfare (education, medical care, housing, etc)? What are the distinguishing characteristics, if any, of welfare goods? Discuss alternative methods of taking any such characteristics into account.

7. What are the effects of suppressing markets? Illustrate your answer from 'black', 'white', or 'grey' markets in peace and war, in capitalist and communist economies.

8. 'Markets require people to be selfish.' Comment, with examples on both sides of the argument.

9. 'Markets focus attention on material and away from intangible goods such as leisure.' Analyse the arguments for and against.

10. '... an electronic computer simulates the working of the market...' '... the market simulates the computer.' (Professor Oskar Lange, 1967.) Do you agree with either or both of these propositions? Give reasons and examples.

11. (a) '... the Utopians ... invariably explain how, in the cloud-cuckoo lands of their fancy, roast pigeons will in some way fly into the mouths of the comrades, but they omit to show how this miracle is to take place.' (Professor Ludwig von Mises, 1920.)
    (b) 'There are many ways in which socialist economies can make better use of markets than capitalist ones.'
    Explain the point of *both* assertions and give your assessment of the pros and cons of 'market socialism'.

12. 'The professional competence of economists does not extend beyond the analysis of markets and pricing.' Give arguments for and against, with examples from the works of leading writers.

13. (a) 'The economist is concerned with cause-and-effect relations and logical consistency. He has no business to attempt to impose his own value-judgements on others.'
    (b) 'The view that there can be a division of labour with the politicians providing "value-judgements" and experts then advising how to realise them is untenable. The politician would have to know as much as the expert to appreciate where the value-judgements come in and what kind are called for.'
    Discuss, and, if possible, reconcile these two propositions.

14. Could an authoritarian régime use market pricing to serve its own ends rather than those of its people as consumers?

15. 'There is no such thing as a free lunch.' Can you think of exceptions? Can you suggest a pleasanter way of making the same assertion?

16. What is meant by talk of 'the political market'? What are its main advantages and disadvantages? Can you suggest methods by which its working can be improved?

17. What would be the effects of establishing a secondary market in council tenancies? Why are some people opposed to the idea?

18. What are the most useful functions of a 'consumer watch-dog'? Are there any traps it should avoid?

19. 'Exit, voice and loyalty.' Distinguish between these three methods of influencing the quality of service. To what extent are they mutually exclusive?

20. What is meant by the assertion that nationalism is a public good? Is this a useful way of analysing the subject?

21. Discuss the arguments for and against the sale of votes. If you are shocked by the idea of a market in votes, say why.

22. 'Inequalities of income are to be justified only to the extent that their net effect is to increase the welfare of the least well-off.' Discuss.

23. What are the effects of inflation on the operation of markets? Distinguish between creeping, rapid, accelerating and uncertain inflation. To what extent could 'indexation' reduce the distortions?

24. Do the adverse effects on the environment constitute a sufficient case for slowing down economic growth?

25. 'In times of prolonged economic weakness, commercial imagination, initiative and incentive are more urgently required and do more good than "fairly shared" austerity.' Comment.

FURTHER READING

Alchian, Armen A., & Allen, William R., *University Economics: Elements of Inquiry*, Prentice/Hall International, London; Wadsworth Publishing Co. Inc., Belmont, California, 3rd Edn. (Paperback), 1974.

Barry, Brian, *Sociologists, Economists and Democracy*, Collier-Macmillan, 1970.

Breton, Albert, *The Economic Theory of Representative Government*, Macmillan, 1974.

Brittan, Samuel, *Capitalism and the Permissive Society*, Macmillan, 1973.
Second Thoughts on Full Employment Policy, Centre for Policy Studies, 1975.

Downs, Anthony, *An Economic Theory of Democracy*, Harper and Row, 1957.

Foster, C. D., *Public Enterprise*, Fabian Research Series No. 300, 1972.

Friedman, Milton, *Essays in Positive Economics*, University of Chicago Press, 1953.
Capitalism and Freedom, University of Chicago Press, 1962.
Inflation and the 'Natural' Rate of Unemployment, IEA Occasional Paper 44, 1975.

Galbraith, J. K., *The New Industrial State*, Penguin Books, 1969.

Hayek, F. A., *The Constitution of Liberty*, Routledge and Kegan Paul, 1960.
Studies in Philosophy, Politics and Economics, Routledge and Kegan Paul, 1967.

Hirschman, A. O., *Exit, Voice, and Loyalty*, Harvard University Press, Cambridge, Mass., 1970.

Johnson, David B., 'The Charity Market: Theory and Practice', in *The Economics of Charity*, IEA Readings No. 12, Institute of Economic Affairs, 1974.

Johnson, Harry (ed.), *Economic Nationalism in Old and New States*, Allen and Unwin, 1968.

Lindbeck, Assar, *The Political Economy of the New Left*, Harper and Row, 1971.

Meade, James E., *The Intelligent Radical's Guide to Economic Policy*, Allen and Unwin, 1975.

Mishan, E. J., *Welfare Economics: An Assessment*, North Holland Publishing Co., 1969.
Cost Benefit Analysis, Allen and Unwin, 1971.

Niskanen, William A., *Bureaucracy: Servant or Master?*, Hobart Paperback No. 5, Institute of Economic Affairs, 1973.

Nove, Alec, and Nuti, D.M. (eds.), *Socialist Economics*, Penguin Modern Economics Readings, 1972.

Peters, G. H., *Cost-Benefit Analysis and Public Expenditure*, Eaton Paper 8, Institute of Economic Affairs, 3rd Edn., 1973.

Popper, Sir Karl, *The Poverty of Historicism*, Routledge and Kegan Paul, 3rd Edn., 1961.

Schumpeter, Joseph, *Capitalism, Socialism and Democracy*, Unwin University Books, 12th Impression, 1970.

Sen, A. K., *Collective Choice and Social Welfare*, Oliver and Boyd, 1970, especially Chapter 5.

IEA Publications

Subscription Service

An annual subscription to the IEA ensures that all regular publications are sent without further charge immediately on publication—representing a substantial saving.

The cost (including postage) is £10.00 for twelve months (£9.50 if by Banker's Order)—£7.50 for teachers and students; US $30 or equivalent for overseas subscriptions. (There is a subscription form on the back of the leaflet inserted in this publication.)

HOBART PAPERBACKS

1. POLITICALLY IMPOSSIBLE . . . ?
W H HUTT *1971 75p*
' . . . The analysis that Hutt offers is a refreshing and succinct attempt to identify the economic consequences of present trends in welfare expenditure, and the political temptations and attractions he thinks are offered by the alternative policies available.'
John Biffen, MP—The Spectator

2. GOVERNMENT AND THE MARKET ECONOMY
SAMUEL BRITTAN *1971 75p*
[For a selection of reviews of this Paperback, see opposite page.]

3. ROME OR BRUSSELS . . . ?
W R LEWIS *1971 75p*
'It is good to read a long-established 'European' elaborating his doubts about certain aspects of the way in which the Common Market may in future develop . . . Mr Russell Lewis . . . points out the distinction between the founding treaty and the way in which it has been interpreted and developed.'
Leader—The Daily Telegraph

4. A TIGER BY THE TAIL
F A HAYEK *1972 £1.00*
'One economist who has never accepted (the) post-war orthodoxy was F. A. Hayek, whose views, which are based on the "Austrian neo-classical" tradition, have suddenly come back into prominence as a result of a new collection of extracts from his writings published under the apt title *A Tiger by the Tail*.'
Samuel Brittan—Financial Times

5. BUREAUCRACY: SERVANT OR MASTER?
WILLIAM A NISKANEN
with Commentaries by DOUGLAS HOUGHTON, MAURICE KOGAN, NICHOLAS RIDLEY, MP, and IAN SENIOR.
1973 £1.00
'Niskanen argues, with some cogency, that every kind of pressure on a bureau head leads him to maximise his budget.'
Peter Wilsher—Sunday Times

6. THE CAMBRIDGE REVOLUTION: SUCCESS OR FAILURE?
MARK BLAUG *1974 £1.50*
'Professor Blaug seeks to present and assess the ongoing controversy between the so-called "Cambridge School" and the economists of the Massachusetts Institute of Technology and to relate it to "the current 'crisis' in economics". The controversy is over the theories of growth, capital and the determination of income distribution.'
Ian Steedman—The Times Higher Education Supplement

RESEARCH MONOGRAPHS in print

1. *Restrictive Practices in the Building Industry* FRANK KNOX and JOSSLEYN HENNESSY (40p)
2. *Economic Consequences of the Professions* D. S. LEES (40p)
3. *A Self-financing Road System* G. J. ROTH (50p)
4. *Marketing for Central Heating* CHRISTINA FULOP and RALPH HARRIS (30p)
5. *Private Enterprise and Public Emulation:* A study of Italian experience with IRI and lessons for Britain's IRC. MARIO DEAGLIO (30p)
6. *John Stuart Mill's Other Island:* A study of the economic development of Hong Kong. HENRY SMITH (30p)
7. *Source-book on Restrictive Practices in Britain.* Edited by GRAHAM HUTTON, with a Bibliography by JOSSLEYN HENNESSY (60p)
10. *Copyright and the Creative Artist* DENIS THOMAS, with a prelude by A. T. PEACOCK (30p)
12. *Economic Sanctions and Rhodesia* T. CURTIN and D. MURRAY (40p)
13. *Consumers in the Market: A study in choice, competition and sovereignty* CHRISTINA FULOP (50p)
14. *Taxation and Welfare: A report on private opinion and public policy* ARTHUR SELDON (40p)
15. *Integration in Freight Transport* A. A. WALTERS (60p)
16. *Dependency and the Family* MARJORIE BREMNER (40p)
17. *The Shape of Britain's Tariff* SIDNEY J. WELLS (40p)
18. *The Cost of Council Housing* HAMISH GRAY (40p)
19. *Systems Analysis in Social Policy: A critical review* IDA R. HOOS (40p)
21. *The Marketing of Milk* LINDA WHETSTONE (40p)
22. *Social Benefits and Tax Rates* A. R. PREST (30p)
23. *Pitfalls in Econometric Forecasting* E. W. STREISSLER (50p)
24. *Detergents: A Question of Monopoly?* GEORGE POLANYI (50p)
25. *Agricultural Support in Western Europe* RICHARD HOWARTH (40p)
26. *Markets for Employment* CHRISTINA FULOP (60p)
27. *India: Progress or Poverty?* SUDHA R. SHENOY (£1.00)
28. *How Much Unemployment?* JOHN B. WOOD (60p)
29. *A Market for Animal Semen?* LINDA WHETSTONE, HENRY SMITH (50p)
30. *Which Way Monopoly Policy?* GEORGE POLANYI (75p)
31. *How much Inequality?: An inquiry into the 'evidence'.* GEORGE POLANYI, JOHN B. WOOD (£1.00).
32. *How Much Subsidy?* A. R. PREST (50p)

RESEARCH REPORTS in print

Choice in Welfare 1970: Third Report on Knowledge and Preference in Education, Health Services and Pensions. RALPH HARRIS and ARTHUR SELDON. 1971 (£5·25)

A Competitive Cinema TERENCE KELLY with GRAHAM NORTON and GEORGE PERRY. 1966 (£1·00)

9720